How to Retire

Comfortably and

Happy

on Less Money than the
Financial Experts Say You Need

Insider Secrets to Spending Less While Living More

By Connie Brooks

How to Retire Comfortably and Happy on Less Money than the Financial Experts Say You Need: Insider Secrets to Spending Less While Living More

ISBN-13: 978-1-60138-204-7   ISBN-10: 1-60138-204-9

Library of Congress Cataloging-in-Publication Data

Brooks, Connie, 1980-
How to retire comfortably and happy on less money than the financial experts say you need :
insider secrets to spending less while living more / by Connie Brooks.
   p. cm.
Includes bibliographical references and index.
ISBN-13: 978-1-60138-204-7 (alk. paper)
ISBN-10: 1-60138-204-9 (alk. paper)
1. Retirement income--Planning. 2. Finance, Personal. I. Title.
HG179.B7453 2008
332.024'014--dc22

                              2008030045

Printed in the United States

INTERIOR LAYOUT DESIGN: Vickie Taylor • vtaylor@atlantic-pub.com

Printed on Recycled Paper

Dedication

For my husband Allen, our daughter Bella, and our parents: Nancy, Phil, Anita, and Dennie.

We recently lost our beloved pet "Bear," who was not only our best and dearest friend but also the "Vice President of Sunshine" here at Atlantic Publishing. He did not receive a salary but worked tirelessly 24 hours a day to please his parents. Bear was a rescue dog that turned around and showered myself, my wife Sherri, his grandparents Jean, Bob and Nancy and every person and animal he met (maybe not rabbits) with friendship and love. He made a lot of people smile every day.

We wanted you to know that a portion of the profits of this book will be donated to The Humane Society of the United States.

–*Douglas & Sherri Brown*

The Humane Society of the United States ©

The human-animal bond is as old as human history. We cherish our animal companions for their unconditional affection and acceptance. We feel a thrill when we glimpse wild creatures in their natural habitat or in our own backyard.

Unfortunately, the human-animal bond has at times been weakened. Humans have exploited some animal species to the point of extinction.

The Humane Society of the United States makes a difference in the lives of animals here at home and worldwide. The HSUS is dedicated to creating a world where our relationship with animals is guided by compassion. We seek a truly humane society in which animals are respected for their intrinsic value, and where the human-animal bond is strong.

Want to help animals? We have plenty of suggestions. Adopt a pet from a local shelter, join The Humane Society and be a part of our work to help companion animals and wildlife. You will be funding our educational, legislative, investigative and outreach projects in the U.S. and across the globe.

Or perhaps you'd like to make a memorial donation in honor of a pet, friend or relative? You can through our Kindred Spirits program. And if you'd like to contribute in a more structured way, our Planned Giving Office has suggestions about estate planning, annuities, and even gifts of stock that avoid capital gains taxes.

Maybe you have land that you would like to preserve as a lasting habitat for wildlife. Our Wildlife Land Trust can help you. Perhaps the land you want to share is a backyard—that's enough. Our Urban Wildlife Sanctuary Program will show you how to create a habitat for your wild neighbors.

So you see, it's easy to help animals. And The HSUS is here to help.

The Humane Society of the United States
2100 L Street NW
Washington, DC 20037
202-452-1100
www.hsus.org

Table of Contents

Foreword

By Paul Roldan

Managing personal finances for retirement is often a major challenge for most people. Retirement investing is an area of finance typically overlooked because it tends to lack a sense of urgency until later in life. However, those who make it a priority earlier in life rather than later, have a major advantage in their quest to reach financial independence.

Connie Brooks, in *How to Retire Comfortably and Happy on Less Money than the Financial Experts Say You Need*, provides a comprehensive overview on how to properly manage your personal finances for retirement. She has taken timeless financial principles and has communicated them so well anyone can implement them on their own. This book will equip you with the practical tools and knowledge you need to become well prepared for retirement. It is not only critical to take these principles to heart, it is equally important you execute on the advice Connie gives. Your retirement depends on it!

Starting to invest for your retirement sooner rather than later has tremendous implications on your ability to reach financial independence. Use this book to guide you through how to make retirement investing a priority for you and your family. In addition, by being financially disciplined and instituting sound financial principles it will have a significant impact on you and your family's lifestyle for generations to come.

Paul Roldan, Senior Partner
Allgen Financial Services, Inc.
301 E. Pine Street, Suite 150
Orlando, FL 32801
Phone: 407-210-3888
Toll-free: 800-6ALLGEN
888-6ALLGEN
roldan@allgenfinancial.com
www.allgenfinancial.com

Paul Roldan is Co-Founder of Allgen Financial Services, Inc., a financial services firm focused on helping individuals and businesses

better manage their retirement investments. Paul is an undergraduate alumnus of Princeton University and a graduate alumnus of Harvard University.

Paul's career began as a Financial Analyst with the Federal Reserve Bank off Wall Street where he served on the evaluation group for the Orange County Crisis and the Mexican Economic Crisis. Prior to starting Allgen he was an Investment Advisor with Raymond James Financial Services and Equity Services, Inc. He has been an investment advisor since 1996.

"Retirement . . . is when you
stop living at work and begin
working at living."

Unknown

Section 1

Eliminate Your Debt
Before You Retire

"Failing to plan is the same as planning to fail."

~Alan Lakein

Introduction

The choices you make today, tomorrow, and every day will either help you retire or prevent you from doing it.

The earlier you begin planning for retirement, the better off you will be. The longer you wait to plan, the more you will need to save to be financially secure. Some people will take this truth and use it to beat themselves up for not having planned earlier. Others will panic and never face the situation.

You can retire on less than you think you need. It doesn't matter when you start planning. Beginning late is better than never beginning at all.

Whatever your past is — whether you have thousands saved already or are deeply in debt with no retirement plan — you have options. This book shows you how to maximize your returns, minimize your debt, and bring your retirement one step closer.

In this book you will find realistic strategies for saving without sacrificing things you love. Each chapter includes everything from money-saving tips to case studies and recommendations from top financial experts. All are designed to give you practical advice on how to live well for less and retire in comfort.

Having a successful and secure retirement boils down to one simple truth: You are already in the process of retiring.

Your retirement is based on your choices today; in the small day-to-day decisions, as well as in the larger financial ones.

It is never to late to begin planning your retirement. And refusing to plan will only increase your panic and fear. Even if you are already retired, or are on the verge of retirement, the plan you put in place today will lay the foundation for the rest of your life.

Your retirement is a journey, not a destination. It is a journey made easier by having the right tools, some patience, and a willingness to face your fears. Now is the time to take your future into your own hands and plot your course.

Take this book with you as a guide. Use what works for you, and discard what does not. These tips, formulas, and case studies will help you build your own plan for retirement.

This country is headed for a storm in the next few decades. It is a storm that will wash away the security for many Americans who plan to collect Social Security and Medicare. Do not be one of them. The only person responsible for your retirement is you, not the government, not your employer, but you. Social Security and Medicare will be forced to undergo massive changes in the near future. Experts believe these are two of the most likely changes.

- Decreased benefits

- Raising the age required for eligibility

In the long run you will not benefit from these changes. If you are near retirement you may have a few years to receive Social Security benefits, but it is essential to realize that you cannot count on Social Security forever. The older you get, the more likely you are to have costly or unexpected medical expenses. Sadly, people may find government-sponsored programs failing just when they need them the most.

This does not have to be your story. Now is your chance to provide for the future regardless of your timing. Work through the budgeting sections of this book, take stock of your net worth, calculate your future returns, and maximize your investments.

Your retirement is a journey, and it is time to take the next step!

Credit Cards Will Keep You from Retiring

Good retirement advice starts with sound financial advice. If you want to retire someday, you are going to have to build a financial shelter that will weather any storm. You cannot build a secure shelter for your old age on the shifting sands of credit cards, adjustable rate mortgages, and home equity loans.

Four timeless pieces of financial advice that will lay the foundation for your future include:

- Spend less than you earn

- Use credit as a last resort

- Save more than you need to

- Invest for long-term benefits.

If you are approaching retirement and still carrying large balances on your credit cards, a second mortgage, and high auto payments, you are playing dice with your future. In 2005 the Office of the Comptroller of the Currency (OCC) required major credit card companies to raise minimum payments from 2 percent to 4 percent of the total balance on your credit cards.

Imagine for a moment that you retire with a considerable amount of credit card debt. Worse yet, what if you are trying to use your credit cards to compensate for a reduced income during retirement? What is going to happen when you are living on a fixed income, making minimum payments on your cards, and the required payment is raised again?

A 2 percent increase in your minimum payments may not sound like much, until you look at the facts. In 2006 the average American carried up to seven credit cards, owed around $8,000 dollars or more, and paid nearly 15 percent interest on each card. Prior to the increase, minimum payments for $8,000 worth of debt at 15 percent interest totaled about $160 a month. After the 2 percent increase, the minimum payment doubled to $320 a month.

If you choose to carry your credit card debt into retirement, you need to be prepared for something like this. If you cannot handle an increase without dipping into your investments or savings, your retirement years will not be as secure or last as long as planned.

The Magic of Compounding Interest

Credit card companies understand compounding interest. It is their bread and butter, and makes up the bulk of their profit. They understand exactly how compounding interest benefits them, and they are counting on the fact that you do not understand it. Once you understand how compounding interest works, you will want to put it to work for you instead of giving the credit card companies control of your money.

Example #1:

If I gave you a nickel and told you I was going to double the amount that I give you every day for 30 days, how much would you end up with at the end of the month? Would you have $100 dollars? Would you have as much as $400 dollars?

Here is the surprising answer. If the amount I gave you doubled every day, at the end of the month you would have $53.7 million dollars.

This is an exaggerated example, since no investment allows you to double your money reliably every day. The important point is that the new total each day is used to figure out the next day's interest, and the credit card companies take full advantage of this compounding.

This principle works just as well over a long period as it does a short one. Take a look at this example. Instead of investing and earning interest on our own money, we are paying it to credit card companies.

Example #2:

You have a credit card with a $2,000 limit, which you have reached. The interest rate on the credit card is 15 percent, and every month you make the minimum payment required. Pretend for now that you never charge anything else on that card. How long will it take you to repay your $2,000 debt, and how much will you pay in interest?

The answer is this. By making only the minimum payment, say 4 percent of your total balance each month, it will take you 8.7 years to repay the initial $2,000. During that time you can expect to pay $847 dollars in interest to your credit card company. Payments and interest that could have been compounding for you in a savings account are working against you instead.

This is the opposite of financial freedom. If you never learn to put the flow of compound interest on your side, you will never be able to retire comfortably — if you get to retire at all.

Before we move on, let us take a quick look at what would have happened if you had paid off that credit card and put $80 a month into a savings account for the same eight-year period.

Example #3:

You put $80 a month into a savings account with a 4 percent interest rate every month for eight years. At the end of eight years, instead of paying $2,847 to your credit card company, you have $9,033.48 in your savings account.

One method helps you retire; the other one keeps you from retiring. Now that you understand all this, how do you make compounding interest work for you? Eliminate as much of your debt as possible before you retire.

Make your debt earn a spot in your monthly budget. Remember that everything you charge takes you years to pay off, just like your mortgage. You may look at purchasing that pizza, appliance, or outfit differently if you give it the same financial weight as paying off your mortgage. Sometimes it takes just as long to get rid of credit card debt.

For more information on compounding interest and useful debt calculators, go to **www.BankRate.com.**

Using a cash advance option on your credit card is one of the worst mistakes you can make. Cash advances compound interest at a higher rate than other purchases on your credit cards. They are also the last thing your monthly payment is applied to. The credit card company wants to keep that high-interest balance on your card as long as they can. If you take out a cash advance, it will never be paid off until you pay the entire balance on the card.

What Do You Pay Off First?

If you are like most Americans, you have a mortgage — maybe even a second mortgage or a home equity loan. You have credit card debt and chose to finance your vehicles. As you go through this book remember that every year you are in debt is one more year you may have to wait to retire comfortably.

Every year you let your money work for someone else is a year you cannot get back. Compound interest takes advantage of time. Do not wait until it is time to retire to start investing in yourself. Invest now and look forward to the benefits.

This does not mean that people about to retire will not benefit from this strategy. On the contrary, life does not end when you retire. Even if you are on the verge of retirement, you still have many years to reap the benefits of smart investments and less debt. There is no time like today to stop investing in Visa and MasterCard and start investing in your future.

You have several options once you decide to start paying off your debt. Some of them are as simple as writing a check every month until the debt is gone. Others are as complex as transferring balances or taking out a second mortgage and repaying all your cards at once. Only you can decide what fits your situation. If you are in doubt, schedule an appointment with a qualified financial advisor who can help you evaluate your situation. For now, let us take a look at some of the pros and cons of different repayment strategies.

The Straightforward Approach to Debt Repayment

There are a lot of different strategies available to you when you decide to start paying off your debt. The most important thing to remember is to find what works for you. Most experts agree that the following suggestions are the best way to eliminate debt.

- Make a list of all your debt.

- Create a monthly budget.

- Repay the debt with the highest interest rate first.

- Once that debt is paid, move on to the debt with the next highest interest rate and repay it.

- Rinse and repeat.

These are simple, easy strategies. However, if you have little extra money each month to pay down your debts, it could take you a long time to be debt-free. Some financial gurus advocate paying down the smallest balances first. If you choose to do that, be aware that through the magic of compounding interest, this could cost you thousands of dollars over the life of your debt. It is better to get rid of the highest interest rates first, rather than the lowest balances.

Balance Transfers

Credit card companies may offer a 0 percent annual percentage rate (APR) on balance transfers for up to a year. If you cannot get a balance transfer at 0 percent, you may be able to get one at a rate that is less than what you are paying now. Read the fine print to make sure that other fees on the card do not end up costing you more than if you had never transferred your debt.

Make sure you find out how long your introductory rate will last. Mark the date on a calendar, and develop a payment plan that meets the date. If you do not pay down your debt before that time you will have to accept a new higher interest rate when the offer expires, or refinance, yet again.

Lending companies are in business to make as much money as possible. Why do you think they are willing to buy your debt from your current credit card company? It is not because they want to help you. They agree to buy your debt because they want to collect interest on what you owe over the next eight or ten years.

Taking Out a Second Mortgage to Repay Your Credit Cards

This strategy is as risky as it gets. If you refinance the mortgage on your home, you may get a large loan at a decent interest rate, possibly more than enough to repay all your credit cards and maybe even your vehicles. So why not do it? After all, you can save a lot of money in interest and make a single, reduced payment each month.

To this I say to you, "Debtor, know thyself!" If you think there is even a shadow of a doubt that you will be tempted to use those credit cards after you have paid down the balances, avoid doing this at all costs. You could lose your home, ruin your credit, and take years to recover from what seemed an ideal solution. If you are considering this as an option, ask yourself a few questions, and answer them honestly.

- Do you have a cash emergency fund?

- Do you rely on your credit cards for emergencies?

- What will happen when you refinance your mortgage and have large available balances on your credit cards?

- What will you do for birthdays and gifts for Christmas?

- What about holidays like Christmas?

- Will you have the discipline to cut up paid-off credit cards?

If there is the smallest possibility that you will continue to regularly use your credit cards after you pay them off, this option is not for you. Be honest with yourself about your habits. It is easy to convince yourself that you will use those cards responsibly. It is harder to follow through with that promise to yourself.

Do you have enough discipline not to use your paid-off cards? Are willing to bet your home on it? Instead of refinancing your mortgage to pay off credit cards, take out a personal loan if possible, and investigate all other options.

There are times you will want to refinance your credit cards, your house, or your car. If it seems like too much trouble, remember that neglect benefits the creditor, not the debtor. You may want to avoid this challenge because you were turned down the first time, or you just do not have time to fool with it. If you feel this way, you are costing yourself a portion of your hard-earned retirement. Every dollar you spend in interest could have been put to work for you instead of someone else.

You have learned to adjust your life to your debt. What if you were able to lower your debt and invest the excess? It is possible to begin building your retirement just by changing a few old habits and being aware of where your money is going.

Good Habits Build Wealth

We are all creatures of habit. Our financial habits have developed and been reinforced throughout our lives. If you are practicing poor financial habits, you are going to have a poor and uncertain retirement. It takes time to master a new habit, but it gets easier.

Practicing the following habits will help you chart a course to your retirement.

- Create a budget.

- Pay all your bills on time. Mark the due dates on your calendar.

- Identify your long- and short-term goals.

- Talk to your significant other about your plans to be sure you are on the same page.

- Discuss your individual goals for retirement and create a plan together.

- Regularly review the credit offers you get online and in the mail for better terms.

- Shred any mail or statements you do not need to keep.

- Transfer the balances of all your loans to better terms whenever possible.

Your budget is like your investment portfolio. Check it periodically to eliminate risk and to be sure it is still meeting your needs. Make an appointment with yourself and mark your budget review dates on a calendar.

Ask for What You Need

All credit card companies have payment options they do not disclose unless you ask. Policies vary by company, but here are examples of things you can have changed just by calling and being persistent.

Change your due date — If you are constantly late because the due date for your credit cards falls on a date that is not convenient for you, call and ask your credit card company to change it to a date that fits your schedule. Most companies offer several billing dates to fit their customers' needs.

Lower your interest rate — Call your credit card company and tell them you are thinking of transferring your balance to a card with a lower interest rate. Give them the opportunity to keep your business by reducing your APR or by offering you a comparable rate — 0 percent for six months or a year. Companies want to keep your debt and should offer to lower your current rate to stay competitive.

Get your fees removed — Almost all major credit card companies allow their telephone operators to remove fees from your credit cards. The catch is that you have to ask them to do it. You may literally have to say, "Can you remove any fees from this card, please?"

Examples of fees that can be removed include past late fees, over-the-limit fees, and occasionally, membership fees. Every company has their own policy. Some companies allow employees to remove up to one year's worth of fees each year. Other credit card companies may be willing to only remove one such fee once a year. You will not know what your company is willing to do until you call and ask. If they offer to remove only one, ask if they can remove two or three instead. Only persistence is going to help you in this case.

Reduce or eliminate your membership fees — Again, this is something you will have to ask for because it will not be offered. If you are paying a high yearly fee to hold a card, ask about reducing it, waiving it, or eliminating it.

Call back several times if necessary — It may take several calls to get what you want. If you get an unhelpful person on the other end of the line, be polite. If they refuse to help you meet your goals, ask to speak with a manager, or call back and speak with a different operator who has more patience. This is your future and your money we are talking about. You have to take the time and care enough about your finances to do whatever it takes to get the change you need.

Separate Your Emotions from Your Purchases

If you frequently purchase things on credit, you are not making sound financial decisions. There are many way we trick ourselves into believing we should buy items we do not need. Here are some of the most common excuses. Are you telling yourself these lies?

I am entitled to it — Whether it is a big-screen television, a brand-new car, a small appliance, or a new outfit, you worked hard and you have earned the right to purchase it. Entitlement is a tricky concept. Yes, you work hard. You have worked long stressful hours to purchase that item.

My question to you is this, "If you are entitled to X, why are you purchasing it in a way that forces you to pay someone else interest?" By purchasing with credit instead of directly, you are forcing yourself to work even more hours, days, months, and sometimes years just to pay off that purchase. This adds stress to your life and worry to your days. Is that what your hard work is paying for?

A true sense of entitlement comes from having your finances in order; saving for, and then purchasing the item of your dreams. It does not come from taking the quick road to satisfaction and paying for that mistake with months, or even years, of interest.

It will make me happy — It might make you happy for a while. You have to ask yourself what will make you happier; a new iPod, cell phone, or a new washer and dryer; or a well-balanced investment portfolio and a comfortable retirement? What will last and bring you the most satisfaction?

If you invest your money in a new X, will it increase in value over the years? Will it provide you with financial returns that secure your future? You may think that a $20 pair of shoes will make you happy now and not make a difference in your overall financial situation, but it does. Every purchase matters. Every purchase that brings temporary happiness is an empty purchase. Instead, investing that interest could have been used to help provide you with long-term security.

I am not telling you that you can never purchase another pair of shoes or new clothes. Nor am I telling you that you can never use your credit cards; I am telling you to be reasonable in your spending and to keep a healthy credit score.

Your finances can be compared to your weight. If you continually provide your body with food it does not need you will end up overweight and sick. If you continually purchase unnecessary items on credit you will end up in debt. One piece of cake will not make you fat, and one pair of shoes will not bankrupt you. It is not the exception that matters; it is the choice you make every time you pull your wallet out. These choices will allow you to retire comfortably or keep you from retiring at all.

I need it — Do you? Could you borrow it instead? Shop around and get it cheaper? Save for it instead of putting it on a credit card? You can ask yourself six basic questions when deciding whether you need an item:

- Do I use it regularly? If not, can I borrow one instead?

- Will there be an emergency if it breaks? Should I start saving for a replacement as soon as possible to avoid a credit emergency.

- Could I make do with something I already have?

- Do I need a new X, or am I just tired of the old one?

- Am I willing to pay interest so that I can have this today?

- Am I buying this to impress someone else?

Only you can determine what items you need and which you do not. If you do not need an item, the best choice you can make is not to purchase it. If you decide to buy it anyway the best decision is to pay cash. Keep your credit reserves handy for times when you need an item and are short on cash.

Credit Can Be an Asset

Using credit wisely is a difficult challenge. There are so many temptations, and a low monthly payment is a nice way to have all the things you want, right?

It may help to view your investments as a series of dams, pools of money representing a common goal — the safety of your family. Your credit is one pool. If you make bad decisions with your credit, the dam leaks, your money flows out, and risk spills over into other areas of your life. If you make wise choices the dam holds, and that pool of money is available when you need it.

Your retirement is linked to your entire financial picture, not just part of it. Mismanaging any part of your finances will cause your debt to spill over into other parts of your life and threaten your security.

In this day and age, it is unrealistic to tell you to cut up all your credit cards, never charge anything, and go live naked in the woods like a hermit. Credit, particularly your credit score, will determine many of your options in life. The key is to manage it successfully.

Let us look at these examples:

Jane is a single mother, 42 years old, and has a son about to enter college. She makes about $60,000 a year, has good credit with a score of 720, a mortgage on her home, and an auto loan. She has four credit cards and has not charged more than 20 percent of the available credit on any of them. She makes regular, timely payments. Also, Jane has about $5,000 in a savings account. She has no investments other than her 401(k) at work.

When Jane's son, Adam, enters college, she will have many options available to help him pay his school expenses. Her good credit allows her borrowing options she would not have had otherwise. While Jane has not done everything perfectly, by virtue of her good credit score, she will be able to accomplish her immediate goal of putting her son through school.

On the other hand, meet Jason and Emma. Their son is about to enter college also. They are married with a combined income of $90,000, have two auto loans and a mortgage. Their savings account has a balance of $200. In order to pay off their credit card debt, they took a second mortgage on their home. They kept three credit cards after they paid off their original debt, but have reached the maximum on two of them again. When Bob's truck needed tires, the refrigerator broke, and Jane's mother became ill, they used their credit cards to compensate for their lack of cash. Since their second mortgage, they have amassed an additional credit card debt of $12,400.

Now that their son Paul is about to enter college, they will have little support to offer him. Because of their high debt-to-income ratio, few banks will be willing to lend them money for their son's education. Due to several late payments and poor budgeting decisions their credit score is relatively low — 622. If they do manage to get a loan, the interest will be high, and it will add stress to their finances, and perhaps, to their marriage.

If you consider your credit cards and equity in your home a security pool, rather than a supplement to your income, that protection will be there when you need it. If you use them in place of a regular budget and an emergency savings plan, you eliminate important future choices for yourself and your family.

While the goal of this book is to get you to a point where you will not need to borrow money, in retirement or otherwise, the ability to borrow money in a true emergency is valuable.

In these two cases, the best outcome would have been for both families to budget for college long before their children were ready to attend. Life is never perfect, and sometimes even the best laid financial plans fall through. If you make a habit of taking your credit seriously, and buying on credit only in times of extreme need, you will be better prepared when something happens. If you habitually borrow money for things you do not truly need, you are planting seeds of failure for your future.

A heart attack or an illness can keep you from working. What will you do if you have managed your investments poorly and maxed-out your credit before this happens? How will you pay your bills in an emergency if you exhaust all your options in times of plenty?

Keep your available credit safe for times of true need. Make borrowing your last resort, not your first. This will help you weather an unexpected flood instead of drowning in it.

Do You Know Your Credit Score?

Keeping a regular eye on your credit report and your credit score can help you prevent inaccurate information and identity theft. You are entitled to a free yearly copy of your report from all three credit bureaus. Looking at your own credit report does not count as an inquiry, and you can safely do it as often as you want without fear of lowering your score. When was the last time you checked your credit report?

Experian, one of the three credit bureaus, offers a service that allows you to view your credit report online. If you are willing to pay around $12 a month, you can view your credit score any time, and they will notify you of any changes to your report or score as it happens. Having this service is expensive, but it allows you to monitor your credit at any time.

- **Protect yourself from identity theft** — Know immediately if unauthorized accounts are opened in your name.

- **Unauthorized inquiries** — Find out who is checking your report. You can freeze all inquiries until you decide to apply for credit when checking becomes necessary.

- **Challenge incorrect information** — According to the Consumer Federation of America, almost 79 percent of credit reports contain inaccuracies. There is a simple online form to fill out to challenge incorrect information. Removing inaccuracies from your report can help raise your score.

It may help to look at your credit report once a month as you do your bank statement. Reviewing it once a month allows you to protect yourself. Also, there is one more major benefit in knowing your credit score, especially for people with mid to low credit scores. If you know what your score is when you apply for a loan, you can negotiate without applying. If you know your score is a 644, you can be up front with the loan officer and barter rates before you cause an inquiry on your report. For an additional fee per month, you can monitor reports and scores from all three credit bureaus. To learn more about Equifax's online services (Equifax is another of the three major credit bureaus; TransUnion is the third), visit **www.equifax.com.**

It is a common misconception that lenders need your social security number to run your credit report. All they need is your name and address. If you are shopping for a vehicle, a home, or a loan, make sure you do not give them any information until you are ready to permit an inquiry on your report. If you are afraid you will not be able to get a loan, it is always best to know your most recent Fair, Isaac and Company (FICO) scores before you apply. Every lender has a unique set of conditions you will need to meet to qualify. The more informed you are, the less stressful the borrowing process will be.

Even if you do not review your report monthly, you should set a regular schedule each year to review your information and check for inaccuracies. Keeping on top of your credit is an essential step in your retirement process. Just like an annual physical it is not enjoyable, but it is necessary. This is one case where an "ounce of prevention is worth a pound of cure."

How to Raise Your Credit Score

Part of managing your credit is keeping your credit score as high as possible. There is one tried and true method for doing this. Pay your bills on time. By bills, I do not just mean your credit card bills. This includes your mortgage, auto loans, and utilities. Credit card companies can legally raise your interest rate if your utility bills are late. It is called a "universal default policy," and it can come into effect when you pay your utilities late and when your overall debt grows.

Here are other ways to raise your credit score:

- **Give it time** — The longer you pay your bills on time, the more your credit score will rise. Likewise, the longer your hold your accounts in good standing, the more your credit score will rise.

- **Keep your balances low** — In general, charge no more than 15 to 20 percent of your available credit limit. Again, the longer you do this, the better your score will be.

- **Do not open several new accounts at once** — Applying for different credit accounts through several companies at once is known as shopping for credit, and it will lower your score. You can consult several sources for the same loan, and this should not harm your credit score.

- **Remove inaccuracies from your reports** — Incorrect information on your reports will only hurt you when you apply for credit.

Smart financial decisions can also lower your credit score. The banks are in business for themselves, and what is best for you is not often what is best for them. Understand that the following tactics may be what you need to do to overcome your debt, but they may lower your score in the short term:

- **Consolidate your loans** — Having the same amount of debt with fewer open accounts can lower your score. Continuing to make payments on time will raise it again.

- **Close unused accounts** — Closing unused accounts may lower your credit score.

- **Pay off your balances each month** — Credit card companies want to see you carry a revolving balance so they can charge you interest. If you pay your balances in full each month and prevent the interest, it may not lower your score, but it may not raise it either.

When You Should Use Your Credit Cards

If your credit scores are lower than you would like them to be, you should be using your credit cards regularly. The only real way to improve your scores is to use your cards to charge a small amount of money each month and pay off your debt reliably. Credit card companies and banks need to see that you are capable of making regular payments if you want to be qualified for a loan of any sort. People with bad credit often make the mistake of cutting up their cards and never charging anything again. This may be smart financially, but it will keep your credit score low. If improving your scores is one of your overall financial goals, do not charge more than 15 percent of your available credit, and keep making those regular payments. As soon as you meet your goal of raising your scores, discontinue using your cards except in emergency situations. Once your score is high, it will stay high as long as you continue to pay your bills on time.

Eliminating your credit card debt, raising your scores, and actively managing your credit reports are essential first steps on your journey to retirement. Your future is only as secure as you make it. If something beyond your control happens later, the borrowing power you have could be important. Make this part of your foundation as strong as you can today to prevent accessing your sheltered funds sooner than you intend to in retirement.

"The trouble with retirement is that you never get a day off."

Abe Lemons

Simplify Your Life & Save

Your financial solution is as unique as your personal retirement solution. That said, some basic principles can help you provide for yourself and your family without going into debt. Retirement is all about storing away money and investments to be used at a later date. You can apply this principle to your day-to-day life and save your money as well.

If you know you are going to need essential things like clothes, toilet paper, dish detergent, and food, it makes sense to maximize a sale whenever you find one. If you know you are going to need tires or a new car soon, it makes sense to save money in preparation for the event and pay cash.

You can prepare yourself and your family for a smooth day-to-day life as well as a secure retirement. If you have your finances under control, buy extra meat on sale and freeze it. Sell your excess items on eBay to get money back on things you purchased but no longer need. We are going to take a look at a few simple strategies for simplifying your life so you can invest in your retirement.

De-clutter Your Life

Have you ever purchased something you already owned because you could not find it? Do you have a hard time finding a place to put everything? Is your garage stuffed so full of things that you cannot park your car in it? You may have needed the item when you first purchased it, but no longer have a use for it or a place to put it. If so you are not alone. Everyone has experienced something like this at some point in their life. We are afraid to throw anything away because we might need it later? Or, we may have an emotional attachment to it.

A time will come, however, when you realize it is not the things you own in life that make you happy. All the little gadgets and projects you will get to "someday" are not nearly as important as the people around you, and the experiences you have with them. By making financial decisions that invest in your future instead of your present, you will end up with far more comfort than that garage full of stuff will ever provide. If you invest smartly, you will get a nice return on your investment rather than a box full of something that you may need again — eventually.

The goal here is not to get you to throw away everything that you own, but rather to examine each purchase logically right there in the store. Examine each item and ask yourself these questions.

- Do I need this?

- Why do I want this item?

- Do I have a place for this, or will it end up stuffed under a counter or in the garage?

- How soon will I have to replace it?

- Will this item add anything to my life?

- Will anything get better because I bought this?

- Do I have several things like it already?

- Will I regret not saving this money instead?

- Am I buying this just because it is on sale?

- Can I save for this instead of buying it on credit?

If you do this honestly, you will find yourself eliminating many purchases you would normally make without thinking. In Section 2, we are going to look at how to invest all the extra money you will save by cultivating this one simple habit.

Retirement is a process, not a finish line, and it all starts right there in the store. If you buy food or items that you do not end up using, you have wasted an opportunity to set aside some money for your future comfort. Your future comfort could just as easily include a nice sweater or a new car, it is not just for your retirement. Thoughtlessly buying things you do not use prevents you from buying things that make you happy. It robs your security instead of adding to it. It often forces you to pay someone else interest for items that you will never even use which makes it even worse.

The principle of laying away items or money for the future has all but vanished in our culture. When was the last time you put something on lay-a-way instead of purchasing it on a credit card? Most stores do not even offer it as an option any more, but they are happy to offer you a credit card every time you check out.

If you want to retire comfortably, you must change this way of thinking. If you have clutter and excess things in your life, it may be time to get rid of them and pave the way for a new future filled with things you value.

There are several ways to eliminate excess in your home. You can always donate it to charities which will provide a tax deduction. Also, you can consider using today's technology to supplement your finances.

Online organizations like eBay allow you to auction your unused items. This may help you recoup a portion of your original investment in the item and de-clutter your life. Ideally, you should sell on eBay any unused or unnecessary items and put the proceeds toward your retirement funds or credit card balances; a smart way to recapture your investment.

Make no mistake about it, every time you make a purchase, large or small, it is an investment, and some investments are wiser than others. If you have invested in items that are gathering dust in your garage or attic, sell them to help provide yourself with a more secure future. You may not be able to sell everything, but what you do earn is money you did not expect to have. Whether you make $100 or $5,000 doing this, it will be a valuable contribution to your future goals. Any items you are not able to sell can go directly to charity and give you a tax bonus at the end of the year.

For more information on how to get started using eBay, visit **www. eBay.com**. You can also check out the following books, available from **www.amazon.com**, your local bookstore, or your library:

- *eBay for Dummies*, by Marsha Collier

- *The Official eBay Bible, Third Edition*, by Jim Griffith

- *Three Weeks to eBay Profits: Go from Beginner to Successful Seller in Less Than a Month*, by Skip McGrath

Taking the time to consciously simplify your purchases can save you thousands of dollars a year. You can use this money to supplement your retirement savings without completely overhauling your budget to do it.

Your Budget Will Lay the Foundation for Your Retirement

You would not take a vacation without booking a hotel, a flight, and drawing up at least a basic schedule. Planning your trip would be second nature. You might even look forward to the planning because you know what a wonderful time you are going to have on your vacation once you get there.

Your retirement could be the biggest vacation you ever take. Planning it will make all the difference between sipping piña coladas on the beach or being stranded and mugged on the wrong side of town.

Before you can create a successful retirement plan you have to know what you are starting with. Take stock of where you are right now – today. Doing this will help you avoid putting your money into a bad neighborhood. Did you know that you can mug yourself? You can.

You start out with the best intentions of saving for retirement, and all of a sudden, your money gets shanghaied into a new appliance or a new car. You are robbing from yourself, and it happens so easily you hardly even notice.

The best way to prevent this quiet theft of your future is to take a quick look at exactly where your money is going. Now is not the time to make drastic changes to your budget. It is simply time to take a good look at where you are starting so that you can get a clear picture of where you are going. Changes and additions will come later as we discuss ideas to make your money work smarter, and how to optimize your investments.

If you do not have a written budget take the time to sit down and create one. It is nearly impossible to reach your goals if you do not take the time to put them in writing, and make them concrete.

This book contains several budgeting worksheets. You do not have to use them — they are simply a place to start. If you find that pen-and-paper budgeting is tedious and difficult, you might try working with a computerized version instead.

Several excellent budgeting systems are available. QuickBooks software offers you the option to import your information into programs like TurboTax when it is time to file your taxes. Just be sure to evaluate software programs before you make a purchase. They can be expensive, but the time they save may offset the cost and pay for itself at a later date.

An excellent personal-budgeting alternative is called YNAB (You Need a Budget). It has a series of forms to help you keep track of your money as well as tools to help you get out of debt. It includes tools and spreadsheets to help you analyze your mortgage payment strategies and set up a car maintenance schedule. The software is designed to simplify the budgeting process and help you spend less time obsessing over your finances. It costs far less than QuickBooks and other financial software systems.

YNAB is a series of simple spreadsheets that allows you to track your expenses, easily create and maintain a budget, and put your financial savings on auto-pilot. You can find out more about it at **www.YouNeedABudget.com.**

Case Study: You Need a Budget

You Need a Budget (YNAB) is a unique, powerful and proven way to manage your money. It is a personal finance system that allows you to spend less time worrying over your finances than ever before. It allows you to create a living budget that adapts to your current needs. YNAB allows you to set guidelines for every area of your finances easily and quickly, with no worry and no stress.

The You Need a Budget Program also comes with a few excellent bonuses including:

- A debt reduction spreadsheet

- A tax forecaster

- A retirement planner

- A mortgage analyzer

- A car maintenance schedule

For more information on the You Need a Budget program you can visit their Web site at **www. YouNeedABudget.com.**

Until you have a good idea of where your money is going, it will be impossible to make the necessary changes to provide for yourself in your retirement. If you have ever had weeks where it felt like your money was poured out through a sieve, having a budget will stop that.

The other wonderful thing about having a written budget and clearly defined goals is that it allows you to see your progress. You may be feeling overwhelmed about your retirement right now, but if you set reasonable goals and track your progress over several months, you will feel better and will be able to see concrete proof that you are progressing, or not progressing, toward your goals.

De-clutter Your Bills

If you are making several individual payments each month to your utility companies, your bank, and your credit cards, it may help to consolidate them as much as possible. Mark the due dates for each bill on a calendar, and pay them well before the deadlines to avoid extra fees. This alone could save you hundreds of dollars a year. You have a couple of options for simplifying your bill payments each month:

- **Change your due dates** — If you have bills that are due on dates that do not work for you, change them. Call the companies and ask to have the due date moved to one that fits your schedule.

- **Consolidate your loans** — Consider transferring the balances on all your credit cards to one or two with a good interest rate. Again, set the due date to a day of the month that works for you.

- **Set a specific day of the month to pay bills** — Pick a day far enough from your due dates to give the companies enough time to process your payments. Many companies charge a fee to process a phone or Internet payment. Give yourself enough time to mail a check to avoid those fees. Be sure to mark the date on a calendar.

Over time, these tactics will raise your credit score, keep your lights turned on, and eliminate fees designed to take advantage of you. The same goes for managing your checking account. Banks love it when you bounce checks because they get to apply a fee to your account. Having a set time each month to review your bank account and your credit card statements may be boring, but it will keep you from paying money you do not have to pay. Those little fees add up, slowly but surely, just like compound interest.

Consider setting up automatic deposits into your savings account. As little as $10 a week adds up to $5,200 a year before interest. Most banks offer a free automatic deposit service to their customers, and in some cases, you can set this up online.

More banks are offering savings accounts with better interest rates than in the past. This is an excellent option for your emergency funds. Having your funds automatically deposited from your checking to your savings account allows them to grow in a hands-off manner ensuring that you always have something going into savings that you do not have to worry about it. Adding additional money to your savings whenever possible will help you exceed your goals.

You should also be aware of the possibility that your bank offers accounts with better terms than your current account. This is especially true if you have held your account for a long time. If you are still paying a monthly fee for your accounts, you may be able to ask the teller to switch your account to another type or to remove the monthly fees. Why pay your bank more than you have to? You are already lending them your money; why pay a fee for their service? Also consider purchasing your next checks somewhere other than your bank; they traditionally have the highest prices.

Family and Finances: Factoring in Your Children

If you have children, you are well aware of an essential truth; no matter how old they get, they never stop costing you money. My own parents have always made every effort to provide me with all the comfort and security humanly possible, both growing up and in times of need. Now I do the same with my own child. If your children and grandchildren are important factors in your finances, be sure to include them in your budget. If you are still helping your children once they are grown and gone, it makes just as much sense to have a child or grandchild "emergency fund" as it did when they were little.

Even if you have reached the point where you give only Christmas and birthday presents, having that fund in place will allow you to help if you are needed. If you don't use it for the kids, consider it additional emergency money for yourself.

This is the best way I know to keep your children's emergencies from becoming your own. Once you are a parent you are always a parent. Even though your children may be grown and gone, there will be times when you want to help them, especially in case of an emergency.

As parents, we hope our children will not make the same financial mistakes we did, but sometimes, that is unavoidable. If your children or grandchildren are spending money unwisely, and you have some experience in that area, sit down and talk to them about the mistakes you made, and how you overcame those mistakes. That alone is more valuable than any amount of money you will ever provide them.

If you have no children, or even if you do, consider a general "Family and Friends Fund" that can be used to cover everything from an unexpected trip when someone is in the hospital to a birthday that you forgot. Having this money safe and easily accessible will keep you from putting these emergencies on credit. This way you will earn interest in your savings account rather than paying it to your credit card company every time something comes up.

Change Your Habits, Change Your Life

Statistically speaking, only 20 percent of Americans save on a regular basis. Sadly, people cannot get their hands on more than $1,500 in the event of a true emergency. If you are living this way now while you are still working, what is going to happen during retirement?

As you age, the likelihood of high medical expenses and emergencies increases. If you do not develop the habit of saving, you will be left unprepared.

Most of us do not make large, sink-or-swim financial decisions. **We make lots and lots of little ones that cause us to drown.** Changing your financial habits is the key to an easy retirement. It is not about obsessing over your budget or your financial portfolio. Those are tools to get you where you need to go; important tools, but tools just the same. Most of our poor financial decisions stem from the fact that we are not in the habit of setting aside a portion of our income for our future needs.

Your investments and the interest rate on your savings account is important, but it is not as important as **habitually** putting money into investment vehicles.

Put your time and effort into changing the way you think about your life and your financial goals, and then go one step further, put that plan into practice. If you live with your plan, you will never live paycheck to paycheck again, and you will have the retirement of your dreams.

We have become so conditioned to use credit cards and make payments that include outrageous interest, we forget to look at the big picture. It is wonderful that a savings account will pay 6 percent interest, but if you are paying 19 percent interest on a maxed-out credit card every month you are not on the winning end of the deal.

Before you can take the big steps and start investing in your retirement, you first have to start investing in yourself.

Set up an auto-draft from your checking to your savings account, and leave the money there until you have three to six months' worth of expenses. You must have this core savings amount before you can take any risks with your money. Investing before you have accomplished this is foolish. If there were an emergency you would have to have to liquidate, and probably at a loss.

Saving six months' worth of expenses is a daunting task. How do you save that amount of money quickly so you can begin to invest in your retirement?

The answer is deceptively simple — change your habits. If you are eating out frequently; charging anything you want at any given moment; and running down to the wire before your next paycheck; you know immediately where to cut back. It means you have clear areas where you can work to change your habits. All those little changes add up to savings at the end of the month. At the end of a year, they add up to security and a good night's sleep, which you may not have had since you were little.

It is not what you do once in a while that provides for your retirement; it is what you do, or do not do, every day. You are building a secure financial shelter, and it is going to happen one brick at a time. Your habits are the mortar that hold those bricks together and keep the entire house from falling down around you.

How to Change Your Habits

1. **Write down your goals and look at them every day.** Our minds work best when we constantly remind ourselves of what we truly want, not just what we want right now.

2. **Imagine yourself achieving your goals as often as possible.** If your first goal is to set aside six months of expenses for emergencies, visualize checking your bank balance and seeing those numbers. Get your emotions

involved, get excited, and watch how fast that money appears in your savings account.

We often find a way to accomplish things that matter to us, and our financial decisions (good and bad) are often emotionally based. Use this knowledge to your advantage. If you emotionally eat or emotionally shop, it causes negative things to happen. Turn the power of your emotions around to work for you, and get excited about the positive things you want to see in your life.

3. **Set manageable goals.** Unless you win the lottery or receive a large inheritance, chances are your retirement savings are not going to happen overnight. Statistics show that breaking your larger goal down into smaller pieces helps you achieve the end result faster than just focusing on the big prize. Set a goal not to make a charge on your credit cards for a week; send in an extra payment on a debt; or bring your lunch to work instead of buying it. Set a new goal each week if it helps, and practice the old one until it becomes your new habit. Do whatever it takes for you to see the improvement you need in your life.

4. **Celebrate your accomplishments.** You may eventually need six months' worth of expenses set aside, but you can celebrate when you have one month's expenses saved. Do something special to reward yourself and your family for making the right decisions. The hard part about achieving your goals is that it requires consistent effort. You cannot just put a lot of money away at one time; you have to do a little every day.

Rewarding yourself for meeting these day-to-day goals will help you reach the larger ones. Refusing to reward yourself often results in emotional rebellion, and then you are back struggling with your old habits — the destructive ones that made you financially insecure in the first place. If you are staying on your path you deserve regular rewards for doing the right things.

5. **Brainstorm once a week.** Pick a time each week to sit down for five or ten minutes and review the previous week. Then try to come up with at least five more ways you can save money without feeling you are missing out on something. The idea is not to cut out the things you enjoy, but to cut areas where you spend without thinking. Even if it is just for five minutes, it will help you see your progress and give you new ways to save creatively. Make it fun if you can. Pick five things you did well and five things you would like to try next week.

Here is another tip that may help you keep your focus. Surround yourself with a group of financially minded people who are working hard to reach the same goals as you. One of the biggest benefits of the Internet is that you can reach out to others who are just like you even if they happen to be half a world away.

There are many forums, communities, and blogs full of financially minded people. MSN Money is by far the best place to start. **www.MSNMoney.com** features daily thought-provoking financial articles, financial experts, and an active community of readers. You can elect to receive articles in your e-mail inbox each day, offering wonderful insights on investing and suggestions for saving money.

However you decide to go about changing your habits, it is essential that you spend some time on it. It is your regular, habitual decisions that kill your budget and your savings. If you can change those habits by learning to think and react differently, you will find yourself in a better financial position almost overnight, and you will habitually attract wealth instead of rejecting it.

3

The Food Trap –
How to Avoid Eating
Your Retirement

What Are You Eating?

As we age, we begin to realize that fast food, processed foods, and prepackaged foods are hurting our bodies. What you may not be aware of is the way foods we normally consider fresh and unprocessed are treated before we see them. Meat, milk, and eggs are subject to treatment with growth hormones and antibiotics. Much of the fresh produce we consume has been genetically engineered. Our apples are varnished to keep them from browning, and our meat, especially fish, has color injected into it to give it a more appealing look. Cochineal is a common additive used in prepackaged foods. It is made from the bodies of crushed beetles, and is used to add red color to shakes, gelatin, and fruit juice.

With bird flu, mad cow disease, and E. coli poisoning becoming regular events in our news, there is a growing argument for more fresh organic produce and meat to be put on the market. Eating processed foods may not kill us immediately, but they are far less desirable than whole, organic foods raised with a minimum of interference.

The problem with organic food is simple: the cost. Free-range, grain-fed beef is at a premium, and cage-free organic eggs cost almost as much as meat. As you begin your journey toward retirement you are going to have to decide how much of your budget you are willing to spend on quality foods, foods that benefit your body yet match your savings goals.

The good news is that there are many ways to eat well without sacrificing your retirement savings.

Eat Well for Life

Leanne Elys is an expert nutritionist and founder of **www. SavingDinner.com**. She teaches people how to save on food costs using pre-made menus and grocery shopping lists. Using her system and understanding the saving principles behind it helps you save money so you can reach your investment goals.

She is an advocate of what she calls the perpetual pantry system, and offers menus complete with grocery lists to simplify shopping, and help prevent excess purchasing. Visit her Web site to view sample recipes and learn about her perpetual panty — just one example of how she saves money by stocking items her family uses regularly.

Speaking straight from the heart, Leanne gives us her basic advice about eating healthily and how that relationship interacts with the cost of good food:

"Saving money at the grocery store is not all about double coupons and sales. It goes beyond walking out of the store with a receipt that says you saved $25 because you took advantage of a few sales and used several coupons. If what you are buying has ingredients on the label that you cannot pronounce and you do not know what they are, you are not saving anything. It is important to understand that feeding our families is not about filling holes." Leanne says, "We are feeding souls."

The True Cost of Eating Poorly

Your body needs quality foods and sound nutrition to remain healthy throughout your retirement years. Just as the money you are saving provides for your financial reserves, the food you eat today will provide the nutritional reserves you need as you age. Here are a few statistics from Leanne's Web site that you need to be aware of.

- Every 15 minutes, an American woman dies from breast cancer and five others are diagnosed with this disease.

- Heart disease is the number one cause of death in the United States.

- In 2008, nearly 800,000 people in the United States will be diagnosed with diabetes.

Most of these problems can be prevented with proper nutrition. Even though we know that eating well will make us feel better and be healthier, Leanne gets e-mails daily from people who say they cannot afford to eat the way they know they should.

What is Leanne's answer? "We cannot have a cheap attitude when it comes to our family's health. You cannot replace your body. The wear and tear of everyday life is hard enough. When you complicate the issue with negative nutrition, most of the snack foods available at the market, fast food, and convenience foods, our bodies feel it."

Sixteen Ways to Eat Well and Save Money

So how do you eat well and still manage to save money? These simple tactics will help you east well and save money.

1. **Buy only what you need** — Go shopping with your list in hand, and buy only what is on your list. Avoid impulse purchases. Just because something is on sale does not mean you will use it if you buy it and bring it home. If you know what you need before you walk into the store, you will be able to resist the temptation to buy 18 cans of black-eyed peas just because they are on sale.

2. **Clear out your pantry** — Decide what you need for the meals you cook regularly. Do not keep, and do not buy, things you "might" want to use "someday." If that day comes, you can always buy it. The only items worth keeping on hand are ones you use weekly. If your pantry or refrigerator still contains items from 1999, it is time to throw out the expired items and make a fresh start.

3. **Never shop hungry** — If you find yourself at the grocery store after work or ordering pizza because you have no real plan, you are using your hard-earned money to compensate for your lack of planning. It is more cost-effective to have a

regular meal plan that fits your budget. In this case, being prepared can save you thousands of dollars each year.

4. **Grocery shop at off-hours as often as possible** — Most places in the United States offer at least one 24-hour grocery store. Consider shopping after dinner to avoid the post-work rush. Also, avoid shopping on Friday, Saturday, and Sunday if possible.

Stores know that the longer you stay, the more you will buy. Why do you think they line cash register aisles with impulse purchases like magazines and gum? You are just standing there waiting with nothing better to do, and they can often pick your pocket for a few dollars while they have you there.

Stores place items they know you will need, like milk, bread, and eggs, as far from the front door as possible. This forces you to walk all the way through the store, tossing impulse purchases in the cart as you go. Plus, when you shop at peak hours, more people are shopping with you and it takes longer to get through the aisles. This gives you more time to look at things you do not need and possibly buy them. Shopping at off-hours prevents frustration, helps you avoid the long wait to check out, and saves money.

5. **The convenience trap** — It may be faster to run into the local gas station for a gallon of milk, but you pay top dollar for that convenience. It makes more sense to buy extras of those items during your regular shopping than it does to "just stop in" at a place that sells everything at a premium.

6. **Do not buy necessities at the health food store** — They may carry everything from organic apple juice to vegan

macaroni and seaweed, but you may find that the cost of your basic necessities is higher than it needs to be. When you go, buy only what you planned to buy, and beat a path to the door. It may cost you more in gas to shop at multiple stores, but that may be negligible compared to spending $2 to $3 more per item.

7. **Maximize store sales when you can** — If your store is running a special on ground beef and it is one of your staples, buy extra and freeze it for next month. Do this as often as you can for everything you use regularly. If you take the time to plan and invest money in keeping your pantry and freezer stocked, you will find that you have extra money to capitalize on those sales when you run across them.

8. **Shop with cash** — If you leave your debit cards and credit cards at home, you will find that your groceries always fit within your budget. If you take away the temptation to overspend on things you do not need, you will come home with exactly what you planned. What you will not leave with is the added guilt or interest you would be paying just to have a few more boxes of cereal or a few more pounds of meat. It is never a bargain if you have to pay interest on it.

9. **Avoid coupons, if necessary** — In my opinion, coupons are designed for one reason, to get you to purchase things you would not buy otherwise. If you would not buy that item unless you were saving $1.50 on it, you may not need it. If you can find coupons on things you regularly use, they are wonderful. Find out if your store offers "Double Days," where they double your coupons, and plan to shop on those days. "Discount membership cards" that some grocery stores offer are just a polite way of tracking your

purchases to improve their selling tactics. Chances are you can find the same price or lower elsewhere without giving away your personal information.

10. **Avoid price clubs like the plague** – Yes, you can get wonderful deals on things you use often. By "often," I mean a year's supply of potatoes or olive oil. If half the bag rots or the oil goes rancid in six months because you did not need that much of it, you have not saved anything at all. **Buying what you need in quantities you use will always cost you less in the long run.** You may not feel as good about it though. After all, it is exciting to feel like you got a wonderful deal on a valuable item. In the long run you have to decide if saving $4 on all the honey you will ever need benefits you – especially if you do not get a chance to use it before it spoils. The yearly membership fees may even total more than your savings if you do not shop there regularly.

11. **End caps are not always sales** – End caps are the featured items that stores place at the end of each aisle. They usually feature a large sign with the price to make you believe the item is on sale. These items are often things the store has overstocked and would like to see you purchase. Some of them may legitimately be on sale, but others may simply be regularly priced items. We are trained to think that because something is in the middle of an aisle or on a featured display that it is a bargain. Stores take advantage of this mindset and place overstocked items where they will sell quickly.

12. **Larger packages do not always mean you are getting a better deal** – Pay attention to the weight of what you are buying. Every prepackaged item contains the words "packaged by weight." It may also include "contents may

have settled." That is fancy language for "We are putting a smaller quantity into a larger package to make you think you are getting more than you actually get." If you look at the weight difference between the larger packages and the smaller ones, you will often find that the smaller package is really a better deal. Compare prices between the larger and smaller packages, especially if one is on sale and the other is not. Taking the time to compare package weights may seem tedious, but making it a habit will help you get the most for your money every time you shop.

13. **Look for marked-down items in strategic places —** Stores often place deeply discounted items, like damaged boxes, in sections throughout the store. You just have to look for them. Bakery sections may feature week-old pastries or bakery items at rock-bottom prices. If you plan to use them within the week, this is an excellent way to get a deal on something you need without paying full price. Be sure to avoid dented cans because they have their own set of health consequences.

Hostess and Rainbow offer stores in front of their local distribution centers where you can purchase bread and snacks at half the price you would pay in a supermarket. But here is a word to the wise; just because those snack cakes are 25 cents does not mean they are a bargain. Do not get lured into purchasing bottom-of-the-barrel food just because the stores are almost giving it away. Keep your health and wallet in mind when you go in, and be strong.

14. **Buy the loss leaders; avoid the rest —** The sales that stores advertise in the newspaper each week are known as loss leaders. This means the store is taking a loss on those items

to get you in the door. They are counting on the fact that you will purchase far more than that one item when you walk in. It is fine to go into the store, buy only the sale-priced meat or vegetables, and leave. It is not a wasted trip because you only bought two items — it is just the opposite. If you walked in, bought the two sale items you needed, and left, it was money and time well spent — you have wasted nothing at all.

15. Stocking your freezer can save you more than you think — Having a well-stocked freezer is a huge accomplishment. If you fill your freezer with good things, like pre-made meals, meat already in the marinade, homemade egg and cheese burritos, and frozen whole wheat waffles, you are ready for breakfast or dinner with little effort. All you have to do is remove the meat from your freezer the night before and let it thaw and marinate while you worry about other things. Having food ready for you or your family will prevent fast-food runs more than you think and will save money the first month you do it. SavingDinner.com has heart-healthy, low-carbohydrate, and vegetarian freezer menus complete with grocery lists for you to download. Free samples are available for each of the menu options.

If you live alone, using freezer menus can help you as well. Make a family-size meal and freeze it into portions. Then thaw only what you will use at any given time. This keeps you from wasting food, or worse, not cooking at all because "there is no reason to cook just one serving of anything."

16. Store your food well — If you are going to invest in a well-stocked pantry and freezer, be sure that you store the excess as well as possible. If you buy a large bag of chips on sale, use baggies to break the bag down into actual portions. This prevents overeating and keeps your food fresher longer. When you prepare food in advance and freeze it, be sure to spend the extra money for quality zipper-top bags.

Your money will be wasted if your food is ruined before you have a chance to eat it. You can use a combination of aluminum foil and zippered baggies to preserve your meals, and your food will last longer. Label your food with the date you put it in the freezer. That way, you can check it periodically and use anything that may have been in there a while before it spoils.

Your Perpetual Pantry and Your Retirement Accounts

Forming the habit of keeping your pantry stocked is like forming the habit of regularly contributing to a 401(k) or individual retirement account (IRA). You are storing goods that will be there for you when you need them. If you can use the previous methods to trim your food budget, please take the excess and put it toward your retirement. So much of saving for retirement depends on time. You have to put your money away soon enough for the interest it accrues to make a difference. Even if you are close to retirement you can put these strategies to work for you today, and start investing in your future. The longer you wait to do this, the less you will have to show for it in the end. Even if you have only four or five years to put compound interest to work for you, you can save aggressively and reap the benefit in years to come.

Remember to Slow Down

When we come up short it is often because we have been dreading something, and put it off. Slow down each day just a little bit. Many of the financial mistakes we make stem from feeling like we just do not have time: no time to clean, no time to plan a menu, no time to sit down and make a budget, and no time to consider our options for retirement.

You only have 24 hours in each day. If you do not learn to dedicate a portion of today's hours to tomorrow's business, you will always find yourself running behind emotionally and financially.

It is less time-consuming to visit the drive-through than it is to plan a menu and cook a meal. It takes less time to purchase something impulsively than it does to figure out if you can afford it. And it can take a long time to pay for those mistakes.

If you are rushing through your day without taking the time to plan for your future needs, your bottom line is suffering. If you are short on time and want help planning a menu, visit Leanne at **www.SavingDinner.com**. If you are too busy to sort out your retirement goals and your finances, gather everything together and take it to a qualified financial advisor.

When you get right down to it, sometimes it is more responsible to pay someone else to do the work that you do not have time to do. Sometimes you just have to recognize that you do not have to do everything yourself. Your time and your future are worth the investment. You will save far more than you realize by taking the time-consuming details to experts who spend their time handling your issues.

Case Study: Saving Dinner

Leanne Ely is a Certified Nutritional Consultant (CNC) and the owner of SavingDinner.com. Leanne's philosophy is simple: "Make it and they will come." Her mission is to provide simple, nutritious meals that won't break the bank or take large amounts of your time to assemble.

Through her Web site Leanne has reached out to tens of thousands of families across America. She offers a variety of low-cost, healthy meal plans and frozen dinner kits via her weekly Menu-Mailers. She is the author of five best selling cookbooks.

Leanne has been featured in numerous national magazines including *Woman's Day* which cited her as "the expert on family dinners." Her syndicated newspaper column "The Dinner Diva" has been published in newspapers across the U.S.

For more information on Leanne Ely and Saving Dinner you can visit her Web site at **www.SavingDinner.com.**

The Breakfast and Lunch Trap

Packing your own lunch and snacks is an easy way to save a significant amount of money. For example, if you purchase snacks, at an average cost of $1.50, three times a week, and you purchase lunch or breakfast each day, at an average cost of $5, in one year you will have spent more than $1,200 on snacks and meals.

Again, this money could be earning interest in your retirement account. You do not have to start putting away huge amounts. Put away a small amount each day, and it will add up to a comfortable and secure future with little effort. Our days are composed of seconds, minutes, and hours. Over time, they add up to years. If you invest small, regular amounts of money, they will compound throughout the years you have left before you retire. Your retirement is not going to happen with one large amount. You can change your future, one little decision at a time, and one little investment at a time.

Adventures in Monthly Cooking

Cooking once or twice a month may seem like a strange way to plan for retirement, but just like using pre-made menus, the savings will add up faster than you can count.

Monthly cooking requires a freezer and time. It is something you can do in retirement to help keep your costs down and your budget on track. It also means you will have food ready and waiting in case friends or family members drop by or someone gets sick.

These steps are a guide to successful monthly or bimonthly cooking.

- **Cook on the same day every month** – This helps keep your expenses at an expected level and helps you plan your activities as well.

- **Always purchase the Sunday newspaper** – Doing this enables you to clip coupons and watch sales.

- **Keep your food budget under control** – When you see a sale, take advantage of it. If you see a great cut of beef at half the regular price, you can stock up and not worry about the extra expense.

- **Plan your meals** — Otherwise, this is going to be the biggest money sink you have ever seen. If you go to the grocery store with no plan except to buy one month's worth of groceries, watch out. You will be robbing from your savings, not feeding them.

- **Take your written meal plan with you** — Buy only what you need.

- **Grab a friend** — Bulk cooking is an activity easily shared, especially if you live alone. One of you can cook chicken and the other beef. Portion the foods out to match what you need and trade off. This will result in less expense and more fun for everyone. If you can manage to get a group of people to do this, it will work even better. You will have more variety and less work for each person you get involved.

If you are interested in more resources for once-a-month cooking, check these out. The books listed are for purchase at **www. amazon.com**. Check their availability and price at your favorite bookstore; or borrow them from your local library but call first to make sure they have a copy of the book.

Once-a-Month Cooking Resources:

1. *Once-a-Month Cooking, Revised and Expanded: A Proven System for Spending Less Time in the Kitchen and Enjoying Delicious, Homemade Meals Every Day,* by Mary-Beth Lagerborg and Mimi Wilson

2. *Don't Panic — Dinner's in the Freezer: Great-Tasting Meals You Can Make Ahead,* by Susie Martinez, Vanda Howell, and Bonnie Garcia

3. The Everything Meals for a Month Cookbook: Smart Recipes to Help You Plan Ahead, Save Time, and Stay on Budget, by Linda Larsen

4. Frozen Assets Lite and Easy: How to Cook for a Day and Eat for a Month, by Deborah Taylor-Hough

Angel Food Ministries

If you live in the South, you may want to know about Angel Food Ministries. There are no income qualifications. This organization reaches out to anyone who wants or needs to take advantage of a wonderful price on food. They plan the menu, buy the ingredients in bulk, and pass the savings on to you.

There are pros and cons to this. If you enjoy planning your meals, it takes the fun out of it. On the other hand, if you hate planning, hate shopping, and need a real solution, this is for you.

Here is the scoop: For $25 to $30, you get a box of quality food.

Here is the description of the plan from the Angel Food Ministries Web site:

"Generally, one unit of food assists in feeding a family of four for about one week or a single senior citizen for almost a month. The food is all the same high quality one could purchase at a grocery store. There are no second-hand items, no damaged or out-dated goods, no dented cans without labels, no day-old breads, and no produce that is almost too ripe.

"Also offered are specialty boxes, such as steak, chicken, and pork. Many participants in this bonus program appreciate the expanded choices. Additionally, there is no limit to the number of units or bonus foods an individual can receive, and there are no applications to complete or qualifications to which participants must adhere."

This is one way to keep your budget low while still meeting your needs. In the upcoming chapters we are going to focus on how to take the money you are saving, and put it in your retirement fund. Making small changes now will help you retire on far less than you thought.

What Your Food Budget Will Look Like in Retirement

It may seem strange that a chapter on meal planning is included in a retirement book, but food is a major part of your budget each month, and it is one area where you have an opportunity to save money. **The changes you make in your budget now will last for years if you take the time to give it some consideration.** Use the budgeting forms at the end of this chapter to help you determine how much money you need for food.

When you retire, your food budget may or may not change depending on your lifestyle. You may not be going out for lunch as often, but you may want to spend more time socializing with friends at dinner. Unless you are feeding children or relatives who will not be living with you when you retire, your budget may not change at all.

Take the time today to plan your meals and your grocery lists, and you will be amazed at how much money you saved in as little as a month's time.

Your Monthly Food Budget Worksheet

This worksheet is designed to make you think about your food budget. Do you know how much you spend when you shop? If do not plan your menus, you could be putting a crack in your nest egg. Fill this out as a "household" to find out what you are spending.

Which days of the month do you shop regularly?

Usual shopping dates: _____

What is the average amount you spend per planned trip?:

Average expected grocery bill: _____

Number of times per month you plan to shop: _____

Monthly planned grocery budget: _____

How many unexpected trips do you make to the grocery store each week?

Number of unexpected trips per week: _____

What is the average amount you spend per unexpected trip? _____

Total spent per unexpected shopping trip: _____

Estimated weekly total for unplanned trips: _____

Estimated monthly total for unplanned grocery trips: _____

Guess at the average number of items you buy per trip that were not on your list. If you do not have a number, estimate a percentage:

Total and/or percent of unplanned items per trip: _____

How often each week do you eat out?

Total times per week (for everyone) that you ate out: _____

What is the average cost of each of those stops?

Average cost per trip: _____

Average cost per week: _____

Your Monthly Food Budget Worksheet

How often do you purchase soft drinks from somewhere besides the grocery store (e.g., vending machines)?

Average cost of soft drinks per week: _____

Average cost of soft drinks per month: _____

How often each week do you purchase snacks?

Average cost of snacks per week: _____

Average cost of snacks per month: _____

How often do you cook each week? _____

How many people in your household do you feed? _____

How much do you spend total per month (planned and unplanned) at the grocery store?

Monthly grocery total: $ _____

What is the total monthly figure for eating at restaurants (sit-down)?

Total monthly restaurant expense: $ _____

What is your total monthly expense for eating fast food?

Total monthly fast food expense: $ _____

How much do you spend per month on small appliances and cookware?

Small appliances and cookware (planned and unplanned) $ _____

Total monthly amount for food and related expenses: $ _____

Add all your monthly columns together to get this number.

Compare it to the amount you budget for.

Make Your Home Work for You

Is Your Home an Asset or a Liability?

Your home is an investment like any other. It can be one of your biggest assets or a major liability, depending on how you manage it. A smart investor will tell you that becoming emotionally attached to your investments is a sure-fire way to lose money. The same holds true for your home.

At the time you purchased your home, it was undoubtedly the best thing for you to do. You were building equity, perhaps raising a family, and your house provided security and stability. But what happens now that your children are grown and gone?

- Do you find yourself spending money redecorating their rooms?

- Do you charge money to make renovations and end up paying interest on those improvements?

- Have you ever looked at your house and thought, "I just wish there was less maintenance?"

- Are you paying service companies to take care of your lawn or clean you house?

- Do you find yourself shopping to fill up empty space with "things" you purchased?

If you answered yes to any of these questions, moving may make you happier. Your first apartment may have been what you needed at the time, but a growing family and new career changed your needs. You may now realize that your home is too large. If so, why should you pay for space you are not using?

Whether we admit it or not, we put our lives and our finances on auto-pilot and loathe changing them. Our financial habits, good or bad, determine how we spend our days. Do not keep an oversized home out of habit or emotion. Or worse, don't be afraid to finish this stage of your life and enter the next one.

Moving to a Smaller Home Can Have Many Advantages

Depending on your financial situation and financing, you may be able to save money on your current mortgage and taxes.

- You could move closer to your job saving travel time and gas money.

- If you buy a home that fits your need for smaller space, utility bills will not be as expensive.

- If you move to a newer house, there will not be as many repairs, and renovation will not be an issue.

- If you sell your home and move to a smaller, less expensive home, you could use the after-tax profit from the sale of your first home in several ways: apply it to the mortgage on your new home, or pay off high-interest credit cards.

- As you age you may not feel like maintaining your home. The smaller the home, the easier the upkeep, especially if you have health issues.

- Most retirees do not plan to sit at home and fade off into the sunset. If you plan to travel, a smaller home will often cost less to secure and monitor. And it may be less attractive to criminals than a larger home, especially if it is sitting empty.

- Neighborhoods age and change, too. What might have been a wonderful, safe area when you moved there could now be less safe and secure. If you are open to moving, you have the option to choose a new area that fits your needs today.

- Property values in your neighborhood could have gone up or down. If they have increased, you can benefit from that increase when you sell. If they have decreased, you may see more of a gain by selling now. Waiting another ten or twenty years could is a question no one can answer. There is always the possibility the area will decline even more.

Trying to predict what the real estate market will do is impossible. Only you can decide what is right for your situation. If moving is not right for you at this time, you still have options.

How to Reduce Your Mortgage

The following tips are from experts suggesting the smartest ways to reduce your mortgage and the best times to refinance.

- Refinance to a lower interest rate.

- Pay more than you have to each month, even if it is just $10. Over time, the extra money reduces the principal and the mortgage will be paid off sooner, meaning fewer interest payments, too.

- If possible, cancel your private mortgage insurance.

If you purchased your home with less than a 20 percent down payment, chances are you are paying private mortgage insurance (PMI). This is what protects the lender if you default on your loan. Buried deep in the legal vocabulary that you signed when you took out a loan on your home, you should find a PMI cancellation policy.

If you signed your mortgage before July 29, 1999, you can ask to have the PMI canceled once you have paid more than 20 percent of the equity in your home. Homes that were purchased after July 29, 1999, should have automatic termination policies for the private mortgage insurance in place.

If you are not sure you are paying for private mortgage insurance, check your most recent statement. You may have to jump through several hoops, like reappraisal, in order to get it canceled, but you could end up saving thousands for your trouble.

Worksheet: Will Refinancing Benefit You?

If you are considering refinancing your home, this worksheet may help. It takes into account many of the hidden fees. Beware that many individual lenders have additional fees or requirements that may not be included on this form.

Let us look at the projected cost of refinancing your home:

1) Credit report — You are allowed one free credit report a year for your personal use; regardless of whether you run your own report, the lending company will run one for you.

Review your credit reports (all three of them) and scores before applying for this type of loan. You do not want to pay refinancing fees and then be turned down. Have a good idea of where you stand before you begin negotiations.

Total cost to purchase credit reports and scores for you and your spouse: $

2) Loan origination fee — This is a fee that your lender charges you for processing the loan. It is due at the time of closing.

Total loan origination fee: $

3) Application fee — You are charged this fee just for the privilege of applying.

Total application fee: $

4) Discount points — Discount points are fees that you pay to your lender in order to reduce the interest rate. One point equals roughly 1 percent of the total loan amount. By paying more points up front, you can lower the mortgage interest rate for the term of the loan. Points are tax-deductible in the year that you purchase the house.

Total cost of discount points: $

5) Appraisal fee — You may be required to have an appraiser evaluate your property. List the estimated cost here.

Total appraisal fee: $

6) Title examination fee — This should only be included if your lender chooses to have an attorney examine the title in case of a legal question. If it was necessary, include the fee here; if not, skip it.

Total title examination fee: $

7) Title insurance — This insurance policy protects you from legal flaws in your title.

Worksheet: Will Refinancing Benefit You?

Normally, you can purchase the cheapest available insurance, but your lender may have other qualifications.

Total title insurance fee: $ _____

8) Land survey — You may be required to have your home and the surrounding land professionally surveyed when you refinance your home loan.

Total land survey fee: $ _____

9) Document preparation — Your lender charges this fee to prepare your loan documents.

Total document preparation fee: $ _____

10) Legal fees — Should you incur any additional legal expense during the refinancing process, list it here:

Total legal fees: $ _____

11) Add the totals for the entire column to get the total refinancing cost:

Total cost to refinance: $ _____

Will it benefit you to refinance?

1) List your current monthly mortgage payment (principal and interest).

Total current payment: $ _____

2) What will your new mortgage payment be (principal and interest).

Total new payment: $ _____

3) Subtract your new monthly payment from your old monthly payment.

Total difference in payments: $ _____

4) Divide your monthly savings into the total cost of refinancing to equal the number of months it will take to break even: $ _____

You will need to keep the mortgage at least this long for the refinance to be worth the fees.

Biweekly Payments Will Benefit You

If paying down your mortgage sooner rather than later is a priority for you there is a simple way to reach that goal. Consider making biweekly payments on your loan.

If you choose a biweekly payment plan, expect to pay half your monthly mortgage payment every two weeks. This breaks down to 26 payments a year; one every two weeks instead of one a month. That adds up to making an extra month's payment over the course of the year. It also gives you a chance every two weeks to add even a small amount to your payment.

Over the lifetime of the loan, this will add up to thousands of dollars. Biweekly mortgage payments can cut up to eight years off the life of the average loan.

Most lenders will charge a one-time fee for setting up biweekly payments. However, it is well worth it, because you will be making more payments throughout the year and paying off your loan faster.

Avoid companies that charge a fee and offer to set up your biweekly payments for you. It is simple enough to do it yourself, and your lender will have its own fees associated with this. Why pay extra?

The following instructions are the easiest way to get started.

- Grab a copy of your most recent loan statement.

- Grab a folder and label it "Mortgage Agreement" or whatever you like, and keep all your paperwork in this folder until you have your new payment plan set up and running. Keep your folder in an easily remembered place.

- Call your lender and ask for the cash management department. If they do not have one, ask to be directed to someone who can help set up your biweekly payments.

- Once you are sure you have someone who can help you be sure to get their name and direct phone number. Write this information down and keep it in your folder in case you have questions later.

- Set up automatic withdrawals from your checking or savings account. Your lender should be able to do this for you. This is the easiest way to put your payments on auto-pilot. If you cannot or do not want to do this ask your lender what your options are.

- Make sure you tell this person that the extra payments must be applied to the principal of your loan. Otherwise, this will not happen. Your lender will put it in escrow for taxes or insurance if you do not **specifically** tell them not to.

Unfortunately, not all lenders will be able to do "set-up" biweekly payments. They may have outrageous fees for doing it, or they may require you to pay enrollment fees on top of transaction fees. If your lender is not helpful or difficult to deal with you still have options.

One of the easiest way to manage biweekly payments is set up a high-interest savings account just for your mortgage. Every two weeks, put in half of your mortgage payment, plus a little extra. At the end of the month, make your payment from that account.

to supplement your retirement — as long as you are not counting on the value of your home to pay off any other debts.

Historically, relying on your home to do more than house you in retirement can be risky. It is becoming frighteningly commonplace for people to expect equity in their homes to support their excessive credit card debt or their retirement in a way that has real security risks.

Most of us have happily watched our real estate values and their equity climb in recent years. The risk is that real estate can suffer long and frighteningly low periods just as easily as it can balloon into high periods.

The housing market is closely tied to industry and local commerce. If the area is doing well the housing is often doing well. However, the health of local industry and commerce are out of your control. If you are relying on equity in your home as a primary way of getting you through retirement, you may be setting yourself up for failure, or worse, foreclosure.

Unlike stocks, bonds, and other more liquid assets you may end up stuck if you are relying on your house, and the market takes a downturn. It is easy to liquidate a portfolio of stocks and funds. It is more difficult to sell your home, and you are less likely even to try. After all, you are comfortable there — it is your home. This can keep you saddled with a bad debt while the equity in your home decreases.

Reverse Mortgages

A reverse mortgage is a loan to a homeowner who is age 62 or older that allows this person to borrow against the equity in the

At the end of the year send in the extra payment plus any
you have accrued along with a letter to your mortgage co
directing them to apply the extra amount to the princip
For your convenience, a sample letter is included.

Important payment information enclosed

Today's Date

Loan #0000-00-000000

Account/other relevant identifier if necessary # 000000

Your Name
1234 Your Street
City, State Zip

The current payment amount due on [date] is: $[amount]

I am enclosing an additional $[amount] to be applied to the principal.

The total amount of the payment is $[amount].

If you have questions or need to speak to me about this payment, please call [y
name] at 000-000-0000 [cell] or 000-000-0000 [home].

Regards,

Your Name

Your Home After Retirement

You have a unique option available to you after retirement.
plan to remain in the home you currently own, you can co
a "reverse mortgage." This is a way of signing your hom
to the bank until you move or die. In return, the bank
regular payments to you as long as you still live in the
Technically, you retain ownership of the home, but the lo
be repaid immediately if you ever move or when you
settles your bills. This plan is not for everyone, but it can l

home and receive tax-free payments from the lender. Also, the loan does not have to be repaid until you no longer call your house your home, or until you sell your home, move, or die.

With this type loan, the final payment is calculated not to be more than the sale price of your home, and it must be paid by your estate in the event of your death. You retain ownership of your home throughout the life of the loan.

How to know if a reverse mortgage is for you.

- You must be 62 years or older and live in the home for which you are applying for the loan. The older you are, and the more valuable your home is, the more money you receive.

- Most reverse mortgages require no repayment as long as you live in your home. The loan must be repaid in full, along with interest, when the last living borrower dies, sells the home, or moves away.

- The lender is usually a bank, and the normal amount you can borrow is between 20 percent and 60 percent of your home's equity. In exchange, the lender will receive a portion of your home's value when you die or sell the property.

- You have four basic payment options: a lump sum, a regular monthly payment, quarterly installments, or a line of credit you can use when you need it.

- You will still be responsible for property taxes, insurance, and the general upkeep and maintenance of your home. If you do not keep up with these requirements, your loan could be due in full before you are ready.

- If you are close to paying off your mortgage and need the money, this could be a viable option for you, especially if you are not depending on your home to cover your other debt in the event of your death. If you are not in a strong financial position and you die unexpectedly, it could leave your estate in terrible shape.

As you investigate loans clarify exactly what the fees will be. They can vary. Some may be as low as 2 percent of the loan amount or as high as 7 percent. In order to get a lower fee, you may have to deal with a higher interest rate, so do the math carefully as you consider this option.

What you do with the equity in your home is important. Used properly it will provide a large amount of borrowing power in times of true need. Use it carelessly and it is the quick road to financial ruin. Ideally, you want to get to the point where you can pay off or avoid home equity loans entirely. If you max out the equity in your home without good reason, it can keep you from full retirement. Your payments will quickly reach the point where you cannot afford to quit working. Just like any other form of credit, you have to take it seriously and use it as a last resort. Credit works best when you consider it a form of insurance, rather than a quick fix because you were not able to save regularly. Understanding that is one path to true financial independence.

5

Driving Your

Retirement

Your Vehicles

Vehicles can be a lifeline or a liability. How much of one or the other they are depends on your credit score and your average miles per gallon.

The easiest topic to begin with is the benefit of driving a used car. This probably is not your first choice. After all, you work hard, and have earned a nice vehicle. You feel safe and secure driving a new car. But you need to decide if you would rather make a payment on a new car or buy a used one, and put those payments in your retirement account.

Buying a used car will save you thousands of dollars. Those thousands of dollars could be compounding interest in your retirement account and helping provide for your future security.

Older cars cost more to maintain than new ones; are more likely to break down more often; and may have higher repair costs. All of these concerns are legitimate and should be considered.

Most of the advice in this book simply comes down to risk versus reward. If you can do without the security of the perfectly smooth new car, you can reap the benefit of paying thousands of dollars into your retirement fund. If you are willing to carry a cell phone for emergencies, the risk is lowered.

The only one who can make that decision is you. Will it satisfy you more to have a new car and less in your savings? Or will you be happier watching your investment portfolio grow and hearing a few odd noises coming from your vehicle?

Even a car payment of $400 a month results in $4800 per year that could be put towards your retirement savings instead.

Except for the risk of a breakdown — which increases with the age and mileage of the car — older vehicles can be cheaper to own and operate. These are some of the key benefits of owning a used car.

- Save money every month by avoiding a car loan.

- Use the payment savings to help secure your future.

- Obtain lower insurance rates and save more money.

- Save even more by raising the deductible on your collision insurance, or forgo it altogether.

Used Cars and Estimated Repairs

Proactive maintenance is important. Keep the tires rotated, the oil changed, and the antifreeze checked. Have frequent tune-ups, and use quality gasoline whenever possible. This will keep simple wear and tear on an older car to a minimum.

The following list are examples of common repairs based on the mileage of the vehicle.

- Alternator may need to be replaced every 125,000 miles.

- Break rotors should be changed every 80,000 miles.

- Brake drums and calipers last an average of 150,000 miles.

- The clutch should be checked around 75,000 miles.

- Shock absorbers need to be replaced every 75,000 miles.

- Starters last approximately 100,000 miles.

- Timing belts and timing chains have a life expectancy of 100,000 miles.

As you can see, most of these repairs happen between 75,000 and 100,000 miles. Be aware that after 100,000 miles repairs will be more costly. Once you see 140,000 miles everything you replaced at 70,000 miles will need to be replaced again.

Once again, it is risk versus reward. If you have a car in reasonable shape, it may make sense to hang on to it as long as possible. Keep money in savings, and when the repair costs are greater than the cost to purchase a newer car with fewer miles, buy a new car.

How to Purchase a Quality Used Car

Besides doing the obvious, like checking the car's vehicle identification number (VIN) to get the car's history, there are other things you should check before you sign on the dotted line.

The most important thing to remember is to always keep an eye on your bottom line. After all, you are choosing to drive a used car to provide for your retirement and your savings. If you cannot see the direct benefit, do not do it. Likewise, if you are not sure a used car is the right investment for you, do not do it.

If you are considering a used car, treat it like any other investment. You might be able to throw darts at a newspaper to select your stocks, but serious investors research the companies and decide logically whether or not the stock is a good investment.

Purchasing a used car is no different. You should investigate it carefully in order to be sure that the investment is right for you. Like your investment portfolio, it is going to require some predictable maintenance and expense. However, the better your initial pick is, the better off you are going to be down the road.

Tips for finding a used car that can go the distance include:

- Research makes and models online

- Check the paper for local deals and good trade-in options

- After you locate a possible car, check it out, get the VIN number, and then leave to do some additional research

- Check the VIN number yourself. How do you know the used car lot or individual is not lying to you? It is worth the cost to investigate the car if you are going to be driving it for a long time. Log on to **www.CarFax.com** to get started.

Once your potential investment passes the test, call the dealer or the person selling the car and set up an appointment to see it.

Make sure you set up your appointment and check the car as early in the morning as possible. That way you can spot any overnight leakage. Show up for your appointment 15 to 20 minutes early to see if someone is working on the car before your arrival. If it does leak, this person may try to move the car before you can see it.

Take someone you trust with you. When you get in to start the car, have them stand behind it to check for signs of smoke from the tailpipe. If the car smokes, ask them to pay attention to the color of the smoke. Check for smoke before driving the car, and again, after driving the car.

- White smoke — problems in the radiator or the engine.

- Blue smoke — the vehicle is leaking oil.

- Black smoke— fuel pump, carburetor, fuel injector trouble.

When you test drive the car, listen for strange sounds. Check the mileage, the tires, and the steering. Make sure the car does not hesitate when you press on the gas pedal, or idle in a weird way when you stop at a light.

You can do a thorough check for odd noises by taking the car onto the freeway. Roll the window down and drive as close to a median divider as possible. This will cause any noises to echo and be easier to hear. Take the car to a drive-through. It is a good way to hear noises that happen when you idle.

Once you are satisfied with your test drive, park the vehicle for a while and then check it for leaks one last time. Check the tires carefully to be sure the treads are wearing evenly. Examine the car's body thoroughly to look for chips, cracks, or dents in the paint. If you see several dents it could indicate that the car was in an unreported accident.

Check the interior of the car for stains, smells, and water damage. Remember to check under the rugs and under the seats. Most individuals and all car lots will have had the car shampooed recently so you should check under and around the seat crevices for mold or nastier-than-average dirt. You do not want to buy a car that has had water damage because it is impossible to prevent mold. A quick shampoo job might mask it, but a thorough inspection will catch it.

Once you open the hood check the battery for rust, and check the wires and spark plugs to make sure they are not cracked or loose. Ask the owner or dealer if there are any known problems with the car. This works better with individuals than with car lots because individuals owned the car directly. If this person cannot look you in the eye when saying the car is running just fine, have an independent inspection done before you buy it.

Buying a used car is a serious investment. After all, it could save you thousands of dollars, but it could also cost you thousands if you make a poor choice. If you are in doubt, you can always get the owner or lot to have an independent mechanic of your choosing to look over the car before you purchase it.

Some dealers will not want to agree to this. If they argue too much, take your money elsewhere. Having the car independently evaluated can make that risky investment of buying a used car nearly as safe as buying a new one.

If you do not want to have the car evaluated before you purchase it, be sure to have it evaluated as soon as possible after the purchase. It is better to know in advance what kinds of problems you are likely to have rather than to have them appear unexpectedly. For example, if you know the car is going to need new shock absorbers and a tune-up, you can easily budget for them.

Consider a Certified Pre-owned Vehicle

The ideal used car is less than five years old and has fewer than 50,000 miles on it. When you are looking for a used car you should look for one that has been driven no more than 15,000 miles per year. Even if you find one with low mileage it is still not safe to assume it is in great shape; it is just more *likely* to be in great shape.

Certified Pre-owned (CPO) vehicles have been inspected by a manufacturer-trained mechanic and come with extended warranties that are backed by the manufacturer. Many programs throw in extra services. Lexus, for example, provides free roadside assistance and a free loaner car if yours is in the shop.

Choosing to go this route with a used car may still require financing, but the cars are normally newer, with fewer miles, and thus less risk.

Not all programs are fail-safe, however. While some warranties extend several years, others last just a few months. Furthermore, there is always the chance that a shady dealer will try to pass off the worst lemon on the lot as a certified vehicle.

Most CPO programs:

- Only include vehicles that are under five years old

- Have mileage limits of fewer than 100,000 miles

- Only include vehicles that have had no major bodywork from prior accidents

- Refurbish the vehicle after a multistep inspection (75 to 305 inspection points)

- Provide an extended warranty.

Some programs also offer:

- Consumer cash incentives

- Low-interest loans

- Lease programs

- An exchange policy.

If you choose to go with a certified pre-owned vehicle, check the program carefully to be sure you are getting the most benefit for your money. These programs are not unlike credit cards in that some companies offer a reward while others only offer you higher interest rates.

Each CPO program will offer a specific, non-negotiable warranty. The more you know about the type of car you are buying the easier it will be to choose the warranty.

If you know that the particular model you are interested in has a history of maintenance issues, you can buy your warranty accordingly. On the other hand, if you know the vehicle is a model known for its lack of upkeep, you may be able to get by on a less expensive or shorter warranty.

Most CPO programs offer an extended warranty but each one will be different. Be sure to find out whether or not the vehicle still has any of the original warranty left on it, because it should combine with the CPO warranty to give you additional coverage.

Financing a Car

Frankly, it is not a good idea to finance a car unless you have no other choice. Here are a few guidelines to remember if financing is what fits your life.

Have all your questions about paying for the car resolved before you begin to shop. The most difficult part about buying a used car may be figuring out what you can afford. So how do you determine what you can afford?

This is a good rule of thumb. Your monthly auto loan payment should not be more than 20 percent of the money you have available each month after you pay your usual living expenses, rent or mortgage, utilities, food, transportation, credit card payments, and so on. When reviewing your budget take into consideration other associated costs, including fuel, license, registration, personal property taxes, and insurance. Call your insurance company before you purchase the car to determine what the monthly insurance cost will be.

If you are financing a car with a loan figure a down payment of at least 10 percent. If you have enough cash available to boost that percentage, do so. Just because a car lot might offer you the car with no money down, rest assured that you are going to pay through the nose in long-term interest. Cutting the principal of your loan will do more to slash payments than getting a lower interest rate.

If you have bad credit, use the methods in Chapter 1 to help recover your credit now. It can save you a lot of money before you try to finance a car.

Also consider other sources for loans: the credit union where you work, your bank, or other organizations with which you are affiliated. As a last resort, dealers may offer special financing packages for those with credit problems, but you might have to pay as much as four or more percentage points for a loan.

Auto Expenses Worksheets

The following worksheets become especially important if you are driving a used car. They attempt to help you factor in your overall automobile expenses, including the cost of regular maintenance. Taking the time to fill them out will help you understand the true monthly cost of your cars, and may even help you decide if a used car would be a better investment.

Gas Worksheet

Be sure to include boats, recreational vehicles (RVs), motorcycles... anything that uses fuel.

Vehicle #1 $ _____ Miles driven per month _____

Vehicle #2 $ _____ Miles driven per month _____

Vehicle #3 $ _____ Miles driven per month _____

Vehicle #4 $ _____ Miles driven per month _____

Total monthly gas expense: $ _____

Car Payments

List your current vehicle payments here.

Vehicle #1 $ _____ Estimated Payoff Date: _____

Vehicle #2 $ _____ Estimated Payoff Date: _____

Vehicle #3 $ _____ Estimated Payoff Date: _____

Vehicle #4 $ _____ Estimated Payoff Date: _____

Total monthly payments for all vehicles: $ _____

Auto Insurance

If you pay your auto insurance quarterly or yearly, divide the payments by the number of months the payment covers to get your monthly expense.

Example: $6,000/year divided by 12 months = $500/month

Vehicle #1 $ _____

Vehicle #2 $ _____

Vehicle #3 $ _____

Vehicle #4 $ _____

Total monthly gas expense: $ _____

Scheduled Auto Maintenance

Why make it an emergency if it does not have to be? It may seem tiresome to figure this out now, but it could keep you from raiding your savings or your retirement money if you plan for it instead.

Complete this worksheet for all your vehicles to get a total monthly amount that should be saved to cover normal maintenance expenses.

Tires — How many years will it be before you expect to buy tires for this vehicle?

Number of years before you may have to purchase tires: _____

How much do you expect the tires to cost?

Projected cost of the tires: $ _____

Divide the estimated cost of the tires by the number of years away that the purchase is.

Example $800 tires/2 years to save = $400/year

Total yearly cost to plan for tires $ _____

Divide your yearly cost by 12 to see what you need to save monthly.

Example: $400/12 months = $34/month (rounded)

Total monthly expense to plan for tires $ _____

Oil Changes — If you cannot remember the last time you did this, it is time. How many times do you change your oil per year? Every 30,000 miles is the recommended rate.

Number of oil changes per year _____

Total monthly cost of oil changes: $ _____

Tune-ups — Use the same formula as above to plan for your yearly tune-ups.

Average cost of your last tune-up: $ _____

Monthly cost to plan for tune-ups: $ _____

Car Washes — How often do you or your spouse take your cars to be washed?

Monthly cost of car washes: $ _____

Scheduled Auto Maintenance

Parking Permits/Tickets — Only you know your record. If you get a ticket once a year, why not budget it in?

Monthly cost of permits and tickets: $ _____

Public Transportation — List all bus/cab fares or tolls here.

Monthly cost of public transportation: $ _____

Carpool Costs — Add in any costs of carpooling here.

Monthly carpool costs: $ _____

Tax — What are the yearly taxes on your vehicle(s)?

Monthly breakdown of yearly taxes: $ _____

Total Monthly Maintenance Cost — Add all the monthly totals here to see the amount you need to save to prepare for normal vehicle maintenance.

Monthly tire total: $ _____

Monthly oil change total: $ _____

Monthly tune-up total: $ _____

Monthly car wash total: $ _____

Monthly tire savings: $ _____

Monthly tax savings: $ _____

Total monthly auto maintenance cost $ _____

This may seem a large number to save monthly. But if you do save this amount, you will never have to raid an emergency fund for the normal maintenance on your cars again. Just make sure to reserve this money only for your vehicles.

Unless you are using an online bank, like ING Direct, it may be impractical to open up individual accounts for every expense. The easiest way to keep track of how much money you have set aside for each budgeted item is to keep a budget notebook. Use good budgeting software, like YNAB Pro, or mark the new total on your calendar at the end of each month.

If you do the same thing when it comes to holidays and birthdays, you will always be prepared for them. Knowing how much you have set aside for each item will keep you from overspending when you look at your account. And having the money set aside will keep these expenses from becoming credit emergencies.

Section 2

Invest for the Future

Introduction to Investing

Today there are more options than ever when it comes to saving and investing money. If you are not taking the time to research and consider all your financial options you are only cheating yourself. If you know that you are going to earn an average salary of X every year until you retire, the best thing to do is figure out what you can reasonably afford to save, and start saving as soon as possible.

The most important thing you can do, especially if you cannot afford to save as much as you would like, is to be sure that what you do save is earning the best return possible. If you ever hope to retire and live off your savings, you have to be sure that your money is somewhere safe and earning at least enough to beat inflation as you age.

Experts advocate saving at least $1,000,000 prior to retirement. This allows you to withdraw 4 to 5 percent of those investments a year, and ensures that your retirement savings will not expire before you do. But if you are like most Americans, this number is so large it is laughable.

The accepted recommendation is to save 10 percent of what you earn beginning at age 20. The later you begin to save for retirement, the more of your income you will need to save to secure your future. This is undoubtedly good advice for someone 20 years old. What about the rest of us? What happens when you do not begin to save for retirement until you are in your 40s or 50s? Can you still hope to have a secure and comfortable retirement?

Yes — of course you can. You have to begin today, wherever you are, and not let those recommended figures blow you away.

It is true that the older you get before you start saving, the more money you will need to put away. It is also true that beginning today will benefit you more than beginning tomorrow.

Regardless of how old you are or what your savings account looks like, take responsibility. Understand that you cannot go back and change your past behavior, but you can take control of your finances and your retirement starting today. Today is the perfect time to start saving and investing wisely. You cannot get those years back, but you can move forward from here and take advantage of the interest you can accrue in the years you have left. Life does not end in retirement; some say it begins there. The interest your investments are earning becomes especially important once you have retired. So why not do your future self a favor today and explore your options. Get your plan in place, and work toward your goals.

Before you begin investing your money you need to know the basic principles of liquidity and risk.

Liquidity and Risk

Two things affect the interest rates you are offered on your accounts: liquidity and risk. The easier it is for you to get to your money, the less interest you will be paid.

It breaks down like this; the easier it is to get to your money, the lower the interest rate. Low- to no-risk investments earn little to no interest.

The flip side is this; the harder it is to get your money, the more interest you can expect to be paid for lending it. The greater the risk of losing your investment, the higher the return will be.

Knowing these principles allow you to chart your investment course safely. You have to decide what level of risk versus return you are comfortable with, and plan your investment strategy accordingly.

Please do not take that to mean I am directing you to take large risks with your money. I am telling you instead to take only the risks you are comfortable taking and consult with a qualified advisor to work out your individual plan.

The best plan is usually to diversify your risk. Invest the bulk of your money in accounts with less risk or moderate risk, and reserve a few high-risk opportunities for gain, depending on your needs. The later you wait to start, the more aggressive you may need to be. It all depends on where you want to go.

Whatever you do, keep your emergency funds in liquid accounts, like a Federal Deposit Insurance Corporation (FDIC)-insured savings account. This helps protect your investments. Accounts that are tied to the stock market can be volatile.

You do not want your emergency money tied up in an account that has anything to do with the stock market.

For all you know, your emergency could happen at a time when the stock market is at an all-time low. No matter what, you would be forced to pull your money and take a loss.

If your savings are in a protected account, no matter what the stock market is doing, your funds are safe and available to you when you need them.

I have assigned the investments listed in this section a "Risk

Rating" between 1 and 5. A rating of 1 indicates a low-risk investment, while a rating of 5 indicates you need to use money you are willing to lose — disposable income rather than your life savings or retirement money. There are no investments without risk which is why there is no zero rating.

Even if you put your money in your mattress or a hole in the ground you run the risk of fire, burglary, or theft by inflation. There is no completely safe place to put your money. In order to earn interests you have to assume some level of risk. How much risk you are willing to expose yourself to is one of the most difficult decisions you will face as you begin to invest. The end of this section includes information on how to choose a financial advisor. It is my recommendation that you chart your course, choose your prospective investments, and spend about an hour with a couple of different experts, who can tell you if your plan will get you where you want to be by your target date.

It is vitally important that you start a financial journal now before you get too many accounts open, and run into problems managing them. I suggest purchasing a zippered binder that can hold additional papers as well as a notebook. Keep pens or pencils zipped inside so you never have to hunt for one to write down important information.

At the end of each section, I have included a small list that will tell you what to put in your journal in order to keep all your investments straight. Your journal will serve several functions.

It will serve as a record to compare your returns, interest rates, and fees. And you will be able to see at a glance whether your investments are performing as you expected.

It will contain the contact and account information for each of your investments. If you have a question, you can simply flip to that page in your notebook, call your investment company, and you have all the information right in front of you.

If something happens to you, your family will need this record so all your investments will be included in your estate.

When you file your taxes each year, all the information you need will be in one place.

As you begin your journey into wealth and a comfortable retirement, taking the time to manage your investments is just as important as investing. If you do not have time to manage your investments yourself, consult a financial advisor and a good accountant before you open any investment accounts. Hiring someone to manage these things for you from the beginning will be cheaper than all the fees and assorted taxes that come along with mismanaging your accounts.

Once you begin investing regularly, you may be amazed at the number of different accounts you find yourself using. With that in mind, here are a few more tips for keeping everything straight.

Quick Tips for Managing Multiple Accounts

Most of us have trouble managing checking and savings accounts, much less incorporating all the different types of investment accounts and keeping them straight. Mix in all the different contribution limits and tax implications, and you may feel like giving up before you begin. The good news is that it is not as difficult as it seems. The rewards for having these accounts and contributing regularly to them come in many forms. Once you have everything straight, you will be on the path to a peaceful retirement and will sleep better at night.

The trick is to break everything down into manageable chunks of time to keep from becoming frustrated. Rushing into opening any account is a good way to incur unexpected fees and taxes. Do not go out and open every type of account at once. Start by opening one a month or one a year until you are on track. This will give you the time you need to compare offers and decide which investment options are right for you.

There are simple things you can do to keep your accounts in order and avoid unnecessary fees.

Do not open any new accounts until you have investigated at least three competing offers. Once you settle on which company to open your account, read all the fine print. Get a magnifying glass and some aspirin, if necessary, because you will only have to read the agreement once for each account. The last thing you want to have happen is to be hit with unexpected management fees or taxes. Over time, those fees will eat away at your available retirement funds. Do not agree to anything until you are completely certain you understand the terms.

Get a zippered notebook and a safety deposit box. Put the original documents in the safety deposit box and the copies into the zippered binder. The binder should be zippered so that none of your important paperwork falls out. Include all your account information as well as any important insurance information and copies of your wills. In case something happens, it will all be in one place when you need it.

Call each account once a year and ask to have fees waived. It never hurts to ask for what you want. If the companies will not waive them, they may be willing to reduce some of the fees for you as a courtesy. You can put these savings to work by investing them directly back into the account.

Using financial software can also save you time and hassle. No more worrying about losing a slip of paper that had important information on it, and no more stress at tax time when you have to find bank statements, stock statements, and profit/loss worksheets. Having all these accounts can get stressful in a hurry. Having a simple solution to keep track of them is the easiest way to prevent costly mistakes.

If you are not ready to spend money on an accounting program, you can accomplish quite a bit with just a notebook and a pen. Create a page for each investment account, and write down the amount of your contribution each month. Keep it with your other important paperwork, and bring it out when you need it at tax time or to show to your financial advisor and accountant.

While we are going to review the most common investment venues, more investment options than these are available. What follows are simple explanations of the different types of investment accounts. If you have questions, call your investment companies and ask them about their policies. It is your money, and you should know exactly where it is going and how it is working to provide a better future for you.

6

Checking, Savings, & Money Market Accounts

Interest-Bearing Checking Accounts

Risk Rating: 1

Your checking account is the first line of your financial defense. Checking accounts are liquid accounts, meaning you can access your money from anywhere, any time. You have checks and debit cards, and make withdraws from your account regularly. For this reason most banks offer little to no interest, or they require you to maintain a minimum balance in order to earn interest on your investment.

Online banking accounts may allow you to earn interest on your checking account balance with no minimum balance required. Currently, the best of these is the ING Direct Electric Orange ™ Paperless Checking Account. As of this writing ING was offering checking account interest rates between 2.23 percent and 3.93

percent depending on your balance. The advantage with this account is that you earn interest. However, there are two main problems with this type of account for you to consider.

There is no brick-and-mortar bank for you to walk into and talk to someone. The company compensates for this by having an excellent customer service department and 24/7 access to your account and your money.

You have to take several steps to write paper checks from the account. The company attempts to compensate for this by offering an extensive "Online Bill Pay" feature that allows you to electronically pay all your bills. You set it up, and it automatically deducts the money from your account and pays the bill. This is a nice way to automate your finances if you have good control of your checking account. If you do not, having everything automated could cause you to overdraft your account. You are not required to automate your bills with ING Direct. Other options for making payments are available.

You can write electronic checks to people rather than companies through these accounts. The process is simple. You log on, enter the person's information and the amount of the payment. This person will then be sent an e-mail with a link to a page where the account information is entered. The money is then transferred to the person's account electronically. This method can often be faster than writing a paper check because things take less time to clear electronically.

If you need to send a paper check ING also offers this service. You go online and fill out the information. Then they cut the check and put it in the mail for you the next business day. They even offer an overnight service for times when you need to get a paper check there the next day.

One huge plus to this account is that there are no monthly service fees or overdraft fees. If you overdraft your account, ING extends you a temporary line of credit and charges you interest on the amount instead of a flat fee. If you are able to put the money back quickly, this is a better option than the average $35 fee for an overdraft at a normal bank.

You can deposit money into the checking account with a direct deposit from your employer, linking another bank account, or by writing and mailing them a check. ING's debit cards work just like any other bank's, and automatic teller machine (ATM) withdrawals within their 32,000-machine network are free. Fee-free ATMs are available in all 50 states.

This type of account is not for everyone. However, if you are looking for an excellent way to earn interest on your checking account without having a high minimum balance or a lot of fees, this may be for you. You can check out ING's account options at **www.INGDirect.com.**

In the Checking Account page of your financial journal write down the answers for the following information.

- Your account number(s).

- Your personal identification number (PIN) and/or the answer to your security question.

- The telephone number, e-mail address, and physical address of your bank.

- Your bank's hours of operation and if they are open on Saturdays?

- Any fees you will be charged for using the account. Include monthly fees, possible overdraft fees, and your required minimum balance.

- How long it normally takes for deposits to go through and for checks that you write to clear.

- Put copies of any extra paperwork into a folder at the back of your notebook.

Continue to keep your check registry as usual. Having this information handy can help prevent you from bouncing checks accidently, and can allow you to contact your bank at a moment's notice with all of your account information on hand.

High-Yield Savings Accounts

Risk Rating: 1

Savings accounts are slightly less liquid than checking accounts. Banks know you are holding that account with the intent of saving the money, instead of spending it. Because of that, they offer slightly better interest rates and charge no, or low fees on the money you invest with them. Some banks limit the number of transactions you are allowed per month.

Before you begin putting money away for your retirement you must have an emergency fund in place. Once you put your money in an IRA or a 401(k) account you cannot get it back until you retire — at least, not without a hefty penalty. So what happens in an emergency? What happens if you get laid off from work or get sick and have nothing else to fall back on?

The first step to sheltering your retirement savings is to make sure you will not have to access them for any reason other than retirement. This means you must have some form of an emergency savings account.

Many banks are now offering savings accounts with interest rates as high as 4 percent. If you have your emergency funds sitting in an account that is earning 2 or 3 percent interest, transfer your funds to a new account and close the old account.

It does not make financial sense to earn a lesser return on your invested money if you do not have to. Not wanting to take the time to mess with opening a new account, or leaving your money where it is because you are comfortable with your bank, is an emotional decision, not one that is going to benefit you financially.

Keep your emergency savings as accessible as possible. And a traditional savings account with a high interest rate is often the best choice for this. You do need to keep your emergency funds as safe and secure as possible, and savings accounts offer an excellent way to do this and still keep your money accessible at the same time.

FDIC-insured banks that are now offering high-interest accounts include:

- **ING Direct** – Currently, they offer a 3.40 percent interest rate on their accounts, and they have an excellent and supportive customer service department. They also allow you to open multiple accounts for any reason. If you want to have a separate account for your auto expenses or your Christmas expenses, it is easy to set up these accounts and automatically deposit money into them. Visit them on the Internet at **www.INGDirect.com.**

- **HSBC Direct** — They currently offer a 3.55 percent interest rate on their savings accounts. The rate is subject to change, but online banks usually offer better rates. Visit them at **www.HSBCDirect.com.**

- **Emigrant Direct** — They are currently offering a 3.6 percent interest rate on their savings account. Visit them on the Internet at **www.EmigrantDirect.com.**

- **BB&T** — This company currently offers a 4 percent interest rate on their eSavings account. This means that you have to open it up online, but otherwise, it operates exactly as a normal savings account. The BB&T eSavings account may not be available in all areas. BB&T has the added benefit of being a brick-and-mortar bank where you can visit and talk to a teller or manager if you need to. Visit them on the Internet at **www.BBT.com.**

Make sure you research the terms and conditions of each account before committing to one. **You are the only one who can decide what is right for your money and your savings.** If you are in doubt about what to do, please consult an accredited financial advisor. Your retirement, your savings, and your future are complicated issues. Talk with someone, explain your situation, and decide together what is best for you and your family.

In the Savings Account page of your financial journal write down the answers for the following information.

- Your account number(s).

- Your PIN number and/or the answer to your personal security question.

- The contact information for your bank. Include the phone number, e-mail address, and physical address.

- Your bank's hours of operation.

- How long it takes to transfer money from your savings to your checking account.

- The maximum number of transfers you can have in a month without being charged a fee, as well as the fee amount.

- The interest rate on your account. Is it variable or fixed?

- How often you are paid interest on the account. (Daily? Monthly? Every six months?) If it is monthly write down the day that interest is paid. Some banks pay interest on whatever is in the account that day rather than using a monthly average.

- Every time you make a contribution to or a withdrawal from your savings account, write it down on this page along with the date.

- If you make a withdrawal, write down the reason. Over time, this will help you understand where you need to make changes to your budget.

- Be sure to stick some extra deposit tickets in the back of your notebook so that you never have to go without one.

- Put copies of any extra paperwork into a folder at the back of your notebook.

Each year total your cumulative interest paid. This will allow you to see at a glance whether you need to move your money elsewhere to earn a better rate of return.

Money Market Accounts

Risk Rating: 1

Money market accounts combine both features of checking and savings accounts, and usually pay slightly better interest. They are less liquid than checking and savings accounts, and often have strict withdrawal rules.

The following explains the basics of a money market account.

When you open up a money market account at your bank, you are agreeing to lend the bank your money at a certain interest rate. The bank turns around and lends your money at a higher interest rate to make a profit. In return for the loss of liquidity (not being able to withdraw as often as you want to), they pay you a slightly higher interest rate than you would earn from your checking or savings account. This is not the same thing as a money market fund. Money market accounts are FDIC-insured, which means your money is protected if your bank goes under.

The benefits of a money market account include:

- They are offered at most all banks and credit unions

- They often pay better interest than normal savings and checking accounts

- Many investments do not allow checks drawn on your balance. With a money market account you can write a limited number of checks each month.

The normal restrictions for money market accounts include:

- You may need to have a higher minimum balance than a checking or savings account requires

- They have a limited number of withdrawals per month, usually three to six

- You may only be able to write up to three checks per month on your account.

Money Market Funds

Risk Rating: 2

A money market fund is a type of mutual fund that is required by law to make low-risk investments. Companies take your money and invest it in low-risk securities, like certificates of deposit and government securities. They attempt to keep the value of their shares to $1. Ideally, this means that each share will only cost $1 and you will make a profit any time the value rises above this. Money market funds are not FDIC-insured. While they are an extremely low-risk investment, it is possible to lose money by investing in them.

Money market funds are an excellent place to put investment money in the time between buying and selling stocks. But they are not the best long-term investment option, because some high-yield savings accounts can offer almost the same rate of return without the risk. Money market funds often return a rate of around 5 percent, depending on the fund. This is not a guaranteed rate of return, it depends entirely on the management of the fund.

Before investing in a money market fund, treat it like any other stock account. Investigate the fund's prospectus and profile, as well as any other information the company offers.

Two types of money market funds are available: taxable and tax-free. If you purchase shares in a taxable fund, any profit you make is subject to state and federal taxation. Taxable money market accounts have a wide variety of investment options. The fund can invest in anything from certificates of deposit (CDs) to U.S. Treasury securities and more.

Tax-free money market accounts are less common, and the companies can only invest your money in short-term debts issued by tax-free government bodies. Because of this they often earn a lesser return.

When considering which type of fund to invest in, you have to decide whether the lower returns of a tax-free account will provide a greater benefit than the higher-yield, taxable accounts. Taking a close look at their past performance is often the best way to decide. Be aware that in all aspects of the stock market, past performance does not guarantee future results.

Almost all money market funds have management fees. Take a close look at those fees before you agree to them. They may well eat your profits if you do not have a lot of money invested in the account, especially when you factor in that the rate of return is barely above the average high yield savings account.

If you are interested in reading more about the top performing money market accounts, check out **www.iMoneyNet.com** for a list of current leaders.

In the Money Market page of your financial journal write down the answers for the following information.

• Your account number(s).

• The company's contact information and hours of operation.

• The average yield you expect to have.

• If you make a profit, write down the amount. You will need it when you figure your taxes.

• Write down the dates and amounts of your deposits and withdrawals.

• Put copies of any extra paperwork into a folder at the back of your notebook.

Checking accounts, savings accounts, and money market accounts are liquid, low-risk places to keep your money. They will never offer large returns, but they are the best places to keep money that you are going to need quickly. Keep an eye on the interest you are earning with each, and attempt to maximize it whenever possible. Extra interest can only help your money grow. After all, why lend your money to an institution for free? Even if it is easy to access, you should be getting something out of it.

One easy tactic for maximizing your investments is to take the total interest you earn on these types of accounts each year and invest it in something long-term with a better return. It may not seem like much, but it will add up over time just like everything else.

With these types of accounts it is also important to keep a close eye on the fees you are charged. Since there is little profit in keeping your money in liquid accounts the fees become especially relevant.

Once you have your emergency fund in place and you are earning a reasonable amount of interest, it is time to start investing in accounts that offer you a better rate of return. Your emergency fund is what protects your retirement money. If you skip this step, you are planting the seeds of your future in quicksand and not on solid ground.

Certificates of Deposits & Treasury Securities

Certificates of deposit and treasury securities, like bonds and T-bills (treasury bills), are never going to make you a millionaire by themselves. Just like your emergency fund, they exist in your portfolio for one reason alone; to minimize your exposure to risk. They are a fairly secure place to put your money and still tend to perform well even when the stock market is down.

How much money you need to invest in securities will depend on your overall goals for retirement. It is trite but the average rule of thumb is to subtract your age from 100. If you are 30 years old, for example, the traditional advice is to put 70 percent of your money in stock accounts and 30 percent of your money into securities. The older you get the more money you need to move into traditionally secure investments.

At 65 the advice is to only have 35 percent of your investments earning interest in the more volatile stock accounts, and the other 65 percent in slow-growing but stable investments like CDs and bonds. This offers you more protection from the massive ups and downs of the stock market once you prepare to retire.

The traditional advice may not fit your situation. It is simply a bit of wisdom passed down through several generations. Like any good sweeping generalization, it is going to exclude certain situations. If you have waited until you are over 50 to begin saving for retirement, you may want to place more emphasis on a stock-heavy portfolio in order to maximize your gains.

The best thing you can do is plan out what you want to invest in, and try to get a free consultation with a financial advisor. Bring your best plan and let them poke some holes in it so that you can be sure your plan will give you the results you need before you retire.

The chief benefit of adding low-interest securities to your overall portfolio is that they produce a predictable, steady return on your money. It will never be a large return, but you can use the security of that slow, small return to offset some of the larger risks you will take in your stock accounts.

Certificates of Deposit

Risk Rating: 2

Certificates of deposit (CDs) are a more solid account. You commit to lending the bank or institution your money for a specified period, usually a year or more, and they in turn promise to pay you a percentage of interest on the loan. If you pull your money out early, you will have to pay penalty fees. Certificates of deposit are FDIC-insured, so it is as close to a risk-free investment as you can hope for.

Different types of CDs are available. The first is a fixed-rate CD. This means you invest a set amount and are paid a set rate of interest for the duration of the loan. When the CD matures, you collect the principal of your loan plus the accrued interest.

The second type of CD is a variable-rate CD. As the name suggests, the amount of interest you are paid can rise or fall according to different factors that are set by the bank or institution you are buying them from. Some variable-rate CDs have a set plan when the interest rate will rise or fall. Others attempt to track the performance of a specific stock market index like the S&P 500. Read the fine print carefully before you tie up your money. In times of recession, a fixed-rate CD might be a better choice. If your interest rate depends on the stock market and the stock market is down, so are your profits.

The third type of CD is a brokered CD. The terms are similar to fixed- or variable-rate CDs. The only difference is that instead of buying the CD directly through your bank you purchase it through a third-party broker. The big benefit to this is that the broker can shop around and compare rates among banks, then sell you the CD that best fits your needs. The broker may even be able to get you a better rate on your CD than any of your local banks can offer.

If you purchase a brokered CD be certain you know which bank issued it. Verify the legitimacy of the broker and ask them to offer you proof that the CD you are being sold is FDIC-insured. Ask the broker about any management fees or other types of fees that are placed on your account with them. You may be able to earn 2 percent more by using them, but if they charge you the equivalent of that in fees you might as well use your own bank.

The Fine Print

You should understand a few essential things before you purchase a CD:

Some CDs have what is known as a "call feature." This means the bank can cancel the CD if it wants to. For example, you have a CD that pays a high rate of interest and interest rates drop. The bank can then call the CD rather than continue to pay you the higher interest. Read the fine print carefully to be sure you are not purchasing a CD with this feature.

Find out when the CD will mature. You do not want to invest your money in what you think is one year and then find out later the CD's term is for ten years. If you are in doubt about what the fine print means, speak with someone at your bank or brokerage firm who can confirm the exact maturity date and whether or not your CD has a call feature.

Find out when you will be paid interest on your CD. This depends on the bank's policy. Some banks pay monthly while others pay twice a year.

Find out where the interest goes. If you buy the CD from your local bank, they may offer you the option of paying the CD's interest into your checking or savings account, rather than back into the CD. If you intend for the interest to stay there and compound, you will be in for a rude awakening when it starts showing up in your checking account.

Be sure that you understand exactly what the penalties will be if you withdraw your money early. Penalties vary according to the issuing bank's policy.

Ask if the CD has any additional features. Some CDs now offer a "death benefit" that will allow your family to pull the money out penalty-free if you should die before the CD matures.

CDs are an excellent low-risk way to earn a nice return on your money provided you understand the terms. It is important to have CDs as part of your overall portfolio, because there will be years when your stocks and other investments do not do as well as you would like. As long as you have investments like CDs and bonds as part of your investment strategy, they will help offset the risk of your other investments.

When your CDs mature, you can either take the interest they earned and roll it over into your retirement accounts or reinvest the new amount into another CD.

In the CD page of your financial journal, write down the answers for the following information.

- Your account number(s).

- The contact information of your bank or brokerage account.

- The exact amount of the fees you will be charged if you have to pull your money out early.

- The date you purchased the CD, the interest rate, and the maturity date.

- Any options the CD might have: a call feature, a variable rate, or a death benefit.

- The dates you will be paid interest.

- The name of the beneficiary of the CD if something should happen to you.

- Include any account passwords you may need to check the status of your CD.

- Photocopy any necessary paperwork and place it in the back of your journal.

U.S. Treasury Investments

Quite a few options are available for investing in the U.S. Treasury. These are considered secure investments, though they do not always pay high rates of interest. Take a closer look at each of the different types of investment options available to you.

Treasury Bills

Risk Rating: 1

Treasury bills (T-bills) are auctioned and can be purchased directly from the Treasury Department via the Web site at **www. TreasuryDirect.gov** or through brokerage firms. T-bills are issued with maturity dates ranging from a few days up to 26 weeks. They are sold at less than face value, meaning you might pay $950 for a $1,000 bill. When it matures, you get $1,000. The interest is the face value of the bill, minus what you paid for it. In this case you would have earned $50 in interest. The interest rate is set when the bill is auctioned, and there is no call feature, meaning they cannot be canceled by the Treasury Department because interest rates changed. This makes T-bills more secure than CDs in that respect.

T-bills are sold only in increments of $1,000, and there are two ways to bid for them.

1. You can place a noncompetitive bid. This means you accept the terms and interest as they are outlined and ensures you will be able to purchase the bill you want, in the amount you want.

2. You can place a competitive bid through a broker to try to get a better rate of return, but it will not always be accepted.

T-bill profits are exempt from state and local taxes, but federal taxes do apply.

In the T-bills page of your financial journal write down the answers for the following information.

- Your account name and password at TreasuryDirect or your brokerage account.

- The answers to your security questions.

- Photocopy your access card if you signed up with TreasuryDirect.

- The date you purchased the bill and the maturity date.

- The amount you purchased the bill for, and the total amount you will redeem it for.

- Mark the redemption date on a calendar so that you do not forget it.

- Photocopy or print any paperwork you may need to reference later, and put it in the back of your notebook.

Treasury Notes and Bonds

Risk Rating: 1

Treasury notes, also called T-notes, are issued with maturity dates of two, five, and ten years. They require a minimum $1000 investment and can be purchased through TreasuryDirect or a brokerage firm. Treasury notes pay interest every six months until they mature. The purchase price of T-notes depends on several factors. They can be sold below or above face value, depending on the expected interest. For more information on T-notes, go to **www.TreasuryDirect.gov.**

Treasury bonds are long-term bonds that are issued and will not mature for ten to thirty years. Like T-bills and T-notes you can purchase them directly from the government at **www. TreasuryDirect.gov** or through a broker. They are exempt from state and local taxes, and are one of the most secure investments you can make. Treasury bonds require a minimum deposit of $1000. Interest on the bond is paid every six months until it matures. Your purchase price can be greater than, equal to, or less than the actual value of the bond, depending on the expected interest.

Treasury notes, bonds, and bills are examples of extremely secure investments that offer small returns. However, they offer an excellent way to make your overall financial situation more secure. If you begin investing early, you can be more aggressive with your money and invest more in stocks. As you age you are going to want to shift slightly larger portions of your investments into securities where your retirement savings are protected.

In the T-notes or T-bonds page of your financial journal write down the answers for the following information.

- Your account name and password at TreasuryDirect or your brokerage account.

- The answers to your security questions.

- Photocopy your access card if you signed up with TreasuryDirect.

- The date you purchased the bill and the maturity date.

- The amount you purchased the bill for and the total amount you will redeem it for.

- Mark the redemption date on a calendar so that you do not forget it.

- Photocopy or print any paperwork you may need to reference later, and put it in the back of your notebook.

Savings Bonds

Risk Rating: 1

Savings bonds are another form of a secure account that does not earn much interest. Historically, they have barely earned above inflation rates. However, they can be a nice way to incorporate interest and security into your financial portfolio. One of the main advantages to savings bonds is that you can begin investing with as little as $25. Most of the other Treasury securities require $1000 to begin investing. While the rate of return may be small, it is steady and secure.

There are two basic types of savings bonds: Series I and Series EE. Older varieties are labeled E, HH, and H. However, if you purchase them today, you will only be able to choose between I and EE varieties, so we are going to take a quick look at the differences between those two.

The main difference between the two is how they handle inflation. Series I bonds are adjusted for inflation every six months. Series EE bonds are adjusted for inflation just once in their lifetime; when the bond reaches 20 years. Series I bonds began issuing in 1998, and statistically have outperformed Series EE bonds since their inception.

You can purchase savings bonds in several ways. You can go to your bank, which will help you fill out the paperwork and mail it for you. If you do this you will receive your bonds by mail in three to four weeks. You can also go online to **www.TreasuryDirect. gov**, and buy it directly. This site offers electronic bonds and paper bonds. You can buy up to $5,000 total in bonds each year.

If you have paper savings bonds, be sure to keep the actual bonds in a safety deposit box, and put a photocopy of them in your financial journal.

In your Savings Bonds page of your financial journal write down the answers for the following information.

- The date you purchased the bond and its maturity date.

- The amount you purchased the bond for and the amount you will redeem it for once it reaches maturity.

- If you purchased the bonds through TreasuryDirect, write down your account password, answers to security questions, and the information on your access card.

Low-risk securities, like CDs and T-bills, may never comprise the bulk of your financial portfolio, but it is important to have them as part of the total package. The only way to be truly financially secure is to balance risk with safety. If you have a stock-heavy financial portfolio and the stock market is not doing well, it could prevent you from retiring because you will not want to pull your money out and take a loss on your investments.

There is no way to estimate what the market will be doing when it is time for you to retire. Take the time today to start building some low-risk securities into your finances. If you do this now you will be able to retire regardless of what one section of your portfolio is doing.

"Retirement: It's nice to get out of the rat race, but you have to learn to get along with less cheese."

Gene Perret

8

Your 401(k) & IRA Accounts

These two types of accounts are most likely going to form the backbone of your retirement savings. They have definite tax benefits for people who choose to invest in them, and you cannot make up for lost time with either of them because there are yearly contribution limits. That does not mean that you should not contribute to them if you are close to retirement. No matter how close to retirement you are, you can still enjoy the tax benefits, and the longer you wait to start contributing, the less your return is going to be when you retire.

401(k) Accounts

Risk Rating: 3

Basics of 401(k) Accounts

401(k) accounts are retirement accounts set up by your employer to help you save for your retirement. Whatever you contribute to your 401(k) plan is taken out of your check before taxes are assessed. The earnings continue to grow tax-deferred until you begin to withdraw them in retirement. Your employer may match your contributions in a given year.

When you contribute to a traditional 401(k) account your contribution is taken from your check before taxes are assessed. Because you have not paid taxes on the money, the IRS taxes it as you withdraw it during retirement.

You may also have the option of contributing to a Roth 401(k). If you choose to contribute to a Roth 401(k), taxes are taken out of your check first. Then your 401(k) contribution is removed. Because you have already been taxed on the contribution (when you first earned it), you can withdraw the money tax-free from your Roth 401(k) account when you retire. Partially tax-free might be a better statement: you will have to pay interest on any earnings over and above your principal investment.

If you leave your current job, you can roll over your 401(k) into your new employer's account, or you can put it into an IRA. If you cash it out, you will be charged a 10 percent tax for early withdrawal.

When you agree to put money into a 401(k) account, you have as many as 20 different investment options, depending on the company and their individual policies. Some plans even permit "self-directed plans," where you make all the investment decisions. Many offer you the opportunity to invest in your own company's stock. Unless you select a self-directed plan, the administrator your employer has chosen to handle the 401(k) accounts will often take care of the accounting and necessary paperwork for you.

So what does all that mean in English? Simply put, the Internal Revenue Service (IRS) has ensured that your 401(k) or equivalent 403(b) plan is the preferred way to save for retirement. They made it the default choice by allowing you to contribute more to this type of account per year than any other retirement account. The IRS sweetened the deal by encouraging your employer to match at least part of your contributions (hello, free money…). They also allow your money to grow tax-free until you retire and begin withdrawing it.

Unfortunately, less than two-thirds of employees participate in their employer's 401(k) plan. If you are not currently participating and you could be, take a look at a few reasons why you should consider it.

Benefits of a 401(k) Account

Four major benefits to participating in a 401(k) plan at work include:

- Your employer may match your contributions up to a set amount that they decide — can be looked at as free money.

- You can contribute more to a 401(k) plan per year than you can to an IRA account. You can only contribute $4,000 per year ($5,000 if you are 50 or older) per year to an IRA. But you can contribute as much as $15,500 a year ($20,000 if you are 50 or older) to your 401(k). This will end up being the bulk of your retirement if you invest in it faithfully.

- The money is taken out of your check and invested in the 401(k) account before your taxes are figured. If you are borderline between two tax brackets, these contributions could be enough to shift you into the lower one.

- You do have to pay taxes when you begin to withdraw money from your 401(k) account. But it is likely that once you retire you will be in a lower income bracket, and the tax deferral has become a benefit.

Your individual 401(k) benefits are going to depend on your employer. Some businesses make it as simple as signing up and letting the company handle the details; others are now allowing you complete authority over what your money is invested in. If you are interested in maximizing your 401(k) returns, set aside time to talk with your human resources department. Ask them for copies of all relevant paperwork, and read it carefully.

Most 401(k) funds are automatically invested in low-risk securities: bonds, bond funds (mutual funds that buy bonds instead of stocks), and in some cases, blue chip stocks. These investments are safe, but they will not have large returns.

If your company allows you to have some say about where your money goes, chances are you can make more by taking control of your 401(k), as long as you are willing to do the research. After all, this is your retirement we are talking about, and a company, no matter how skilled at managing funds they may be, will never care as much about your retirement as you do. That being said, if you do not research your stocks carefully, and take the reins away from fund managers who do this for a living, you can lose your retirement in a hurry.

You have to decide what is best for you and your family. Taking the time to investigate stocks that your company invests you in is a great place to start. Make sure you understand why they choose to invest your money there to begin with before you move it.

Roth 401(k) Accounts

Employers first began offering Roth 401(k) plans in January 2006. Presently, only about 15 percent of employers offer them, but that number is expected to grow. Roth 401(k) plans work in a similar way to Roth IRA accounts. Both allow you to contribute to the accounts with your after-tax income, and both allow you to make tax-free withdrawals when you retire. This means that taxes are taken out of your check before they take out your Roth 401(k) contribution, so you do not get an immediate benefit, as you do with the normal 401(k). However, the ability to withdraw your money tax-free at retirement is attractive. Roth IRA accounts also have income limits whereas a Roth 401(k) does not. No matter how much money you make, you are eligible to participate in a Roth 401(k) plan.

Remember these two things when considering a Roth 401(k) plan.

- If your employer offers a regular 401(k) plan and a Roth 401(k) plan, you can open both accounts. But you cannot contribute more than a total of $15,500 a year between the two accounts.

- If you have a Roth 401(k) account and your employer matches any part of your contribution, the money they match will be put into a normal 401(k) account, not your Roth 401(k) account.

What If You Need Your Money Before Retirement?

Removing funds from your retirement accounts is a bad idea unless you are faced with a medical emergency or your home is in foreclosure proceedings. But it is your money, and you need to know how to get it out of these funds when you need it.

Most 401(k) plans allow loans and hardship withdrawals before your retirement age. Also, you can start or stop contributions anytime you need to.

401(k) Loans

More than 80 percent of 401(k) plans have a loan system in place. This means you can borrow money for any reason using your 401(k) as collateral. Normally, you are allowed to take out a loan for up to half of the amount in your 401(k) account, up to $50,000. The interest rates on the loan are normally the prime rate plus 1 to 2 percent. When you pay the loan back, the principal and the interest go back into your account.

If you take out a loan against your 401(k), you normally have five years to pay it back and you cannot borrow money more often than once a year. But pay attention to these three warnings.

1. If you do not pay the loan back on time, you will have to pay a 10 percent early-withdrawal tax on the amount you withdrew.

2. If you leave your job with a loan in effect, you have only 60 days to pay the loan back before you are hit with the 10 percent tax.

3. By repaying the loan over a five-year period, you lose valuable time for your money to compound tax-free. You can never make up lost time. Even if you put back every cent of the money you borrow, you will not have as much as if you had never taken it out in the first place.

Hardship Withdrawals

Hardship withdrawals are the other government-approved ways to withdraw your 401(k) money early, but it is not easy to qualify for one. 401(k) plans are not required to make hardship provisions, but most do.

Things that will qualify you for a hardship withdrawal from your 401(k) account (these reasons apply to you, your spouse, and your children) include:

- Certain approved medical expenses

- Purchasing a home

- Educational expenses and tuition

- Preventing the foreclosure of your current home or an eviction

- Approved repairs to your current home

- Burial or funeral expenses.

It is difficult to get approved for a hardship withdrawal for any reasons other than these reasons, and you must provide documentation backing up your claims. Hardship withdrawals are still subject to a 10 percent penalty plus tax. In the event of your death, your estate can withdraw your funds penalty-free. In the event of a disability that prevents you from working, you may be able to withdraw your funds without paying a penalty fee.

If you have questions about your 401(k) account, start by visiting your human resources department or by calling the customer service department of the investment firm that handles the account. You can also visit **www.401k.org** for more information.

401(k) Contribution Limits and Withdrawals

As of 2008, you can contribute up to $15,500 per year, or 100 percent of your salary (whichever is less).

If you are over the age of 50, you are allowed to make an additional "catch-up" contribution of $5,000 per year.

You may begin penalty-free withdrawals from your 401(k) plan at the age of 59 and a half. If you withdraw prior to this age, you will incur a 10 percent penalty on your withdrawals.

Special Tax Considerations for a 401(k) Account

Saver's Credit

If your income is less than $26,000 alone or $53,000 with your spouse, you may be entitled to the saver's credit. This gives you up to a $1,000 credit on your taxes when you contribute to a 401(k),

403(b), 457 plan, Savings Incentive Match Plan for Employees of Small Employers (SIMPLE), traditional IRA, or Roth IRA account. The amount of the credit you will receive depends on the amount of your contributions to these types of accounts in the year for which you are filing taxes. The credit ranges from 10 to 50 cents on each dollar that you contribute up to $1000 in 2008.

The facts are simple, if your employer offers a 401(k) plan, get into it fast. This is true no matter how old you are even if you have fewer than ten years until retirement. Every dollar you save now, in any form, will help you later on.

Even if you plan to leave your current employer, you have options that will allow you to roll the money over into another account without penalty. Because you are allowed so save so much more in a 401(k) account than in an IRA, it is the fastest and easiest way to jump-start your retirement savings. Because the money comes out of your check before you see it, a 401(k) has become one of the easiest ways to save without thinking about it.

Rolling Over Your 401(k) Account

If you are contributing to a 401(k) account and you need to leave your current job, you may choose to roll over your current 401(k) account into a different account that is not managed by your former employer. You can roll it over into your new employer's 401(k) plan, your IRA account, or an annuity account.

If you have invested more than $3,500 in your 401(k) plan, most companies will allow you to leave your money where it is, even if you change jobs. If you are happy with the way your money is being managed, the best choice may be to just leave it alone.

If you want to move your money, the best option is to roll the old account over into your new employer's 401(k) account, with one warning. When the company that was managing your 401(k) writes you a check, it must be made out to the company managing your new 401(k) account. Otherwise, it is subject to taxes and early withdrawal penalties.

If your new employer does not offer a 401(k) plan, your next best bet is to move it into your individual retirement account or annuity account.

Whatever you choose, be prepared to spend time with a financial advisor, who can help you stay within the tax laws and avoid penalties.

In the 401(k) page of your financial journal, write down the answers to the following information.

- The phone number of your human resources department.

- The contact information for the financial company managing your investments.

- Your 401(k) account numbers.

- Any passwords or security questions that are needed to access your account.

- Every time you make a contribution, write down the date and the amount.

Individual Retirement Accounts

Risk Rating: 3

There are two types of IRA accounts: a traditional IRA and a Roth IRA. Both have different advantages and disadvantages and you will have to decide what is right for you. If you are unsure about which account will benefit you most, consult a financial advisor who can look closely at your individual situation and make a recommendation.

How do IRA Accounts Work?

IRA accounts encompass a mix of stocks, bonds, and/or mutual funds. They are investments, and as such, are not guaranteed against loss. If you choose to control your IRA investments rather than having them professionally managed (as in a mutual fund), you will have to do the necessary research to be sure that you are making the right investment choices to fit your circumstances.

Traditionally, investors are given this advice: take more risk when you are young, and move your money into less risky investments with a lower rate of return as you age. If you are 20 and just beginning to invest your money, it may be all right to have two or more index funds, a bond fund, and riskier investments in several individual companies (all these investments are discussed in detail in the upcoming chapters). This will help you see your large gains early on so that your investments can compound to even larger amounts over time. Having more money to invest earlier will always benefit you more than having large amounts later, because investments take time to grow.

No matter what age you are, it is essential that you develop the habit of putting money into your retirement accounts regularly. If it is at all possible, have your deposits automatically withdrawn on a regular basis. Set it on auto-pilot, and do not worry about it, except for rebalancing the money in your portfolio once or twice a year.

Traditional IRA Accounts

A traditional IRA allows you to make tax-deductible contributions throughout your lifetime. You can invest the money in stocks, mutual funds, and bonds, and the earnings will grow tax-free until you begin withdrawal during retirement.

This means you can take a tax deduction for every year you contribute. It also means you will pay taxes when you begin to withdraw money from the account. Since many retirees find themselves in a lower tax bracket after retirement, this is a good option. It lets you to take the tax deduction early, and allows you to contribute more money sooner. The earlier you contribute money to a retirement account, the longer it will have to grow and the greater your returns will be at retirement.

You may begin withdrawing money from your traditional IRA at 59 and a half without incurring a penalty. If you withdraw it prior to this time, you face a 10 percent penalty. You are required to start withdrawing funds from your traditional IRA account by April of the year after you turn 70 and a half.

Traditional IRAs are available to everyone, regardless of their maximum income, and they are an excellent addition to your overall financial portfolio. If you contribute the maximum $5,000 amount to an IRA for even ten years, you will have $50,000 when you reach retirement before any returns are factored in. It may not be enough to live on the rest of your life, but it will help supplement your income and give you added security once you stop working. If you are starting out a little younger, the future is even brighter. If you are in your 30s and begin making your maximum contributions, you could have well over $150,000 at retirement before you figure in any interest or gains.

The best retirement plan should include your employer's 401(k) plan and your individual retirement account. If you have the discipline to make your maximum contributions to each account from age 30 onward, you will retire with over half a million dollars set aside. Again, that is before any compounding or interest is figured in, so if your investments do well, you will have far more.

Roth IRAs

Contributions to a Roth IRA account are not tax-deductible. There are, however, several clear benefits to having this type of account instead of a traditional IRA. For one, when you reach 59 and a half and you begin to withdraw money from a Roth IRA account, your withdrawals are tax-free. There is also no age at which you are required to begin withdrawing money from your account. If you do not need the money, you can let your investments grow as long as possible.

Unlike traditional IRAs, you can wait until you are in your 80s or older before you begin taking money out, and there is no penalty. Every year you are able to put off withdrawing from these accounts will allow your investments to earn you even more money. This is especially important for those who wait until they are almost ready to retire to begin saving for it. You can contribute as much as possible each year and let it grow as long as possible; this will help provide you with additional security as you age.

Another wonderful benefit of a Roth IRA is that you can withdraw your funds penalty-free before you are 59 and a half. There is one exception: You can only withdraw your principal deposits without penalty. You may not withdraw any gains, or you will face the standard 10 percent early withdrawal fee. For example, if you invest $100 in stock, and in five years it is worth $300, you can only withdraw your initial $100 deposit without penalty. If you want to touch the other $200 you are stuck with the 10 percent tax. If you wait to withdraw your funds until you have reached the qualified retirement age (59 and a half), both the principal and the gains may be withdrawn tax-free.

The downside to a Roth IRA is that not everyone will be able to contribute to one. Roth IRAs are only available to individuals earning less than $116,000 a year and couples earning less than $169,000 a year. If you earn more than this, you must contribute to a traditional IRA instead. As you near the upper end of the cut-off incomes, the amount you are allowed to contribute is phased out.

Special Tax Considerations for IRA Accounts

Addenda, provisos, and restrictions do apply where Roth IRAs are concerned. Tax laws seem to be written in Greek for the entertainment of the IRS, but they are easy enough to navigate once you know the rules. As far as your Roth IRA account is concerned here is what you need to know.

You cannot contribute money to an IRA if you did not earn any money that year. Income derived from investments does not count — it has to come from a job. There are special provisions for households where one spouse works and the other does not. As long as you file a joint tax return, the working spouse can contribute to an IRA account for the non-working spouse.

You can never put more money than you make in a year into your IRA. The IRS does not like this, and they will wonder where the extra money came from.

You can apply your IRA contributions to the previous year right up until the time you file your taxes in April of the following year. This means that if you did not meet your maximum before January, you can still keep contributing until April and count it towards the previous year when you file your taxes.

If you withdraw money from your traditional IRA account before you reach 59 and a half, you will be hit with a 10 percent early withdrawal tax. The Roth IRA is an exception, because you can withdraw the original amount of your investment (but not anything it has earned) without paying the 10 percent tax.

Getting Around the 10 Percent Tax

While the idea behind retirement funds is to leave your retirement money in them, situations could arise that cause you to need that money sooner than you planned. If that is the case, there are legitimate reasons where the IRS will allow you to pull money out of your retirement accounts.

There is one rule you must follow. The money must have been in your account for five tax years (not calendar) before you attempt to withdraw it for any of these reasons. Otherwise, you will face the 10 percent tax, even though it was a legitimate reason.

1. **The first-time purchase of a home** — If you have never owned a home before and need to pull money out of your retirement account to purchase one — that is allowed. You can only pull out a lifetime amount up to $10,000 for this reason, so be careful.

2. **Paying back taxes** — If you owe money to the IRS, you can pay them back out of your retirement account.

3. **Permanent disability** — If you are injured permanently, and unable to work, you may withdraw your money from your IRA account without penalty, as long as the money has been in your account for at least five years.

4. **Your death** — When you die, your family may withdraw your funds as part of your estate.

5. **Medical bills** — If your out-of-pocket medical expenses total more than 7.5 percent of your adjusted gross income, you can withdraw money from your retirement account to help cover the costs.

6. **College** — With certain restrictions, you can withdraw money from your IRA account to cover the cost of college for yourself, your children, or your grandchildren. Seek out a financial advisor if you plan to do this to make sure you do indeed qualify.

SEPP: The Other Early Withdrawal Option

There is one other way to tap into your retirement accounts early without penalty. Substantially Equal Periodic Payments (SEPP). This is sometimes known as a 72(t) exemption, named for the section of tax code in which it is found.

Under this section of code, you must take equal periodic payments out of your IRA account for five years or until you reach age 59 and a half, whichever is longer. You will also have to wait a minimum of five years and one day from your first SEPP withdrawal before you are allowed to make unlimited withdrawals from your IRA at 59 and a half. Otherwise, the IRS will charge you the 10 percent tax plus retroactive interest.

The amount of your periodic payment is calculated based on the balance of your IRA account on December 31 of the year before you begin to withdraw money.

You do need to be aware that companies target this loophole. They will do their best to convince you that withdrawing money from your IRA account using periodic payments is in your best interest. To give you one example, Citigroup Global Markets was forced to pay the Financial Industry Regulatory Authority (FINRA) more than 15 million dollars because they conducted "misleading" seminars, that telling people that they could afford to retire early by making SEPP withdrawals instead of waiting until 59 and a half to withdraw their savings. Other companies encourage you to use SEPP withdrawals to invest in real estate.

You might as well invest in a pyramid scheme. These companies do not have your best financial interests in mind just their own bottom line. Unless you have an unavoidable reason to pull these funds out of your retirement account, do not do it. Let that money stay there and do what you intended it to do in the first place: give you a secure future and a comfortable retirement. Be wary of anyone who tells you they can make you rich quickly — that is the first rule of investing.

IRA Contribution Limits

Regardless of whether you choose to open a traditional IRA or a Roth IRA, the IRS imposes limits on how much you can contribute per year. You are allowed to have both types of IRA accounts, but as far as the maximum contribution is concerned, they are considered one account. For example, in 2008, you are allowed to contribute up to $5,000 to your IRA accounts. (The limit is $6,000 if you are over the age of 50.) You can open both accounts and contribute $3,000 to the Roth IRA and $2,000 to the traditional IRA, but you cannot contribute $5,000 to each of them.

What If You Contribute Too Much?

If you are currently contributing to a Roth IRA and your yearly income unexpectedly exceeds the allowable amount ($116,000 for individuals and $169,000 for couples), you are going to have to shift your money around or face a 6 percent excess-contribution tax. The tax will be assessed every year until you get rid of the extra contribution.

The simplest way to fix the mistake is to withdraw the excess amount plus any income you earned on it. You will still have to pay the 10 percent early withdrawal penalty on the income, but you will not have to fill out any extra paperwork at tax time. Ten percent on the earned income likely will still be less than 6 percent of the total contribution.

If you would like to avoid all penalties and taxes you have one other option. You can "re-characterize" the contribution, which involves rolling the extra contribution, plus any income it earned, into a traditional IRA account.

In either case, it is prudent to sit down with a qualified accountant or financial advisor, who can help you solve the problem in the best way possible.

Although the laws and restrictions are complicated, 401(k) accounts and IRA accounts are essential to a secure retirement.

If you are serious about your retirement, your first goal after establishing an emergency fund is to begin contributing to a 401(k) plan if possible, as well as an IRA account that meets your needs. Because there are contribution caps, you can never go back and "catch up" if you do not invest one year. Even if you are about to retire, it will benefit you to go ahead and open one of these accounts and contribute to it. It is never too late to start investing wisely and preparing for your future.

If you are within the income limits, open up a Roth IRA account and defer taking payments out of it as long as possible. Even if you are close to retirement, your investments could still have ten or twenty years to grow. That is plenty of time to see gains that will keep you comfortable well into your old age.

In the IRA page of your financial journal, write down the following:

"The maximum I can contribute to all my IRA accounts, as of 2008, is $5,000 a year. If I am over 50, I can contribute up to $6,000 a year. By law, I cannot contribute more than this amount in a given year."

You will also need to keep these things handy.

- The type of account, traditional or Roth.

- The account numbers.

- The contact information for the company you are invested through.

- Every time you make a contribution, list the amount, the date, and the confirmation number.

- If you sell a stock, write down the amount it was purchased for, the amount it sold for, how long you owned the stock, and any brokerage fees you were charged next to the date. This will make your taxes much easier to do.

- Write down any management fees your company charges you and the dates on which they will charge you.

- Write down how those fees are to be paid. Are they automatically withdrawn from your checking account? If so, this will be a nasty surprise if you do not expect it.

9

Investing in the Stock Market

What Are Stocks?

When you purchase a stock, you purchase a small share of a company. This share entitles you to a portion of the company's assets and profits. The more shares you hold, the greater your claim on the company's profits. When you pool your money with others and invest in the company, you become a shareholder. Owning the company's stock may entitle you to cast a vote equal to the number of shares you own when it comes time to elect the next board of directors. The big benefit to owning stock in a company is this, when the company does well the price of its stock rises, it pays dividends, and the investors profit. The downside is that if the company does poorly, you will not be paid dividends. It is possible to lose your entire investment if the company goes under or declares bankruptcy.

Investors normally do not have a say in the company's day-to-day operations and management decisions, but do assume risks by choosing to invest money with that company. Again, you choose between risk and reward. Companies that are established and have shown a regular rise in profits are a less risky place to invest your money. However, the potential for return is diminished because the company has most likely grown to the point that large gains in stock value are out of the question.

Another name for lower-risk companies like these are "blue chip stocks": Disney or General Electric (GE), for example. These are large, well-established companies with high stock prices that have historically offered a nice rate of return, without much fluctuation. Other blue chip stocks include: Wal-Mart, Coca-Cola, Gillette, Berkshire Hathaway, and Exxon-Mobile.

The problem with investing in individual companies is simple; when you put all your investments in one place and the stock tanks, you lose your retirement. The smarter choice is to invest in mutual funds, index funds, or exchange traded funds (ETFs).

Mutual Funds

Risk Rating: 3-4

Mutual funds are professionally managed funds where groups of investors pool their money and pay a company to manage their investments. Mutual funds also hope to beat the stock market's average rate of return on your investments. Sometimes this involves frequent buying and selling. The mutual fund manager makes the decision when to buy and sell.

Mutual funds are often diversified, meaning the managers invest in large numbers of companies rather than two or three individual companies. When the fund managers purchase stock, they purchase on behalf of their investors and divide the stock among them. When dividends are paid to managers, they divide the profits among all the investors.

This is an excellent way to begin investing. You reap immediate benefits in lower trading costs and make an investment in a large number of companies at one time. **Mutual funds always have management fees and take a percentage of your profits.** This is a "hands-off" form of investing because you do not directly manage the buying and selling of your stocks. Instead, a professional mutual fund manager makes those decisions.

Mutual funds often include a mix of value stocks: blue chip stocks, bonds, and growth stocks. The fund managers hope to maximize growth and minimize risk for their investors.

Index Funds

Risk Rating: 3-4

Index funds are mutual funds that aim to match the performance of a specific stock market index. For example, the S&P 500 Index funds purchase stocks from all 500 companies in the Standard and Poor's (S&P) index. Index fund managers track the market closely rather than trying to outperform it. This means less buying and selling of stocks, fewer capital gains taxes, and lower fees than professionally managed mutual funds.

Exchange Traded Funds

Risk Rating: 3-4

ETFs are index funds that are traded on the stock market. Common exchange traded funds include the Nasdaq-100 Index

Tracking Stock (QQQ), which tracks the Nasdaq-100, and Standard & Poor's Depositary Receipts (SPY), which tracks the S&P 500.

Index funds have opened up new options for investors, because they do not require you to pay the high fees that mutual funds require. Over time those fees can add up and rob you of a significant portion of your profits. By the time you figure in the interest that could have been compounding on those fees, or the other investments you could have made had you not been paying the fund manager, you begin to realize that unless your mutual fund is outperforming the market by a long shot, you are losing money.

Capital gains taxes are the taxes you pay whenever you sell a stock at a profit. Index stocks are only sold if the stock is removed from an index. With mutual funds, the manager is trying to time the market with your stocks, which can result in your paying taxes for every stock that is sold. "Buy and hold rather than buy and sell" is the index fund philosophy.

Over the long term, the S&P 500 index has beaten about 65 to 80 percent of mutual funds, depending on the length of time. It is my belief that this is due to less active management and no attempt to time the market: You purchase the stock and allow it time to grow. Mutual fund managers are only human, and sometimes their best attempts to time the market results in a loss. Most index funds still have fees, but they are often less than the fees charged by managed mutual funds.

Bonds

Risk Rating : 2-3

When you purchase a bond, you are lending money to the government, federal agency, municipality, or corporation. In return for the loan, you are repaid the value of your initial loan plus a set amount of interest. This is done over a set period of time. The end of the loan is known as the date the bond matures.

Types of available bonds include corporate bonds, mortgage and asset bonds, federal agency securities, and government bonds. Bonds are a secure form of investing, but often offer little return on the initial investment. While you have them, your money quietly and predictably earns a set rate of interest.

Bond Funds

Risk Rating: 3

Bond funds primarily invest only in various types of bonds, and can be used to create an additional income for you during your retirement. Bond funds can be complex, so you may want to consider having this area of your portfolio professionally managed. Bond fund managers take care of your funds and write you checks on what is often a monthly basis.

Bond funds can be divided into three basic types:

1. **Short-term funds** — The investments in a short-term fund will mature within two years.

2. **Intermediate funds** — The investments in intermediate funds mature between two and ten years.

3. **Long-term funds** — Long-term funds have ten years or more as their maturity dates.

Should you decide on this investment, it is a good idea to have several different bond funds in your portfolio with staggered maturity dates to ensure a steady stream of income and minimize your risk.

Individual Stocks

Risk Rating: 5

When you choose to purchase stock in only one company rather than an index or mutual fund that encompasses a number of individual companies, you assume the greatest risk of all. You will have to evaluate the company carefully and decide whether this is the best use of your money. This would be something that you do with less than 10 percent of your overall portfolio.

Choosing to invest more than 10 percent of your total financial portfolio into individual stocks can expose your money to unnecessary risks. Make sure that you have everything else in place first before you do this. You need an emergency fund, bond funds, index funds, and everything else secured before you jump into individual investments. Even purchasing blue chip stocks that have historically preformed well is no guarantee that you will see gains by investing in them. Be sure that you have thoroughly researched individual companies before you purchase their stocks.

The Two Theories of Investing

There are two basic investing philosophies, and investors often subscribe to one or the other. The two types of investors have rather rude names for each other, and they enjoy taunting the opposing camps at every opportunity. The first is the "Chicken Little" investor. This person follows carefully every move the stock market makes. He or she focuses on timing the market and buys and sells frequently. They are called "Chicken Littles" because they always believe the sky is falling in one area of the market or another. They attempt to capitalize on these short-term fluctuations as often as possible, with varying degrees of success. In other words, they micromanage their investments.

Chicken Little investors are not content to buy and hold stocks for years at a time — much less decades. They believe that only careful attention to market conditions will bring a profit. These people look down on investors who buy and hold as wasting their money. They tend to make a buy based on rumor and frenzy, and run with the herd. When everyone else sells, so do they.

The second type of investor is called a "Perma-Bull." These investors buy and hold over a long period and believe that no matter what the market does in the short term, given time, it will rebound. They understand that while the stock market fluctuates from day to day, it also has larger fluctuations much like the seasons. They buy stock in companies they research and believe in, and hold the stock for ten years or more to maximize their investments. Often, their decisions run contrary to the herd. When everyone else is buying a stock, they sell that stock at a profit to the new rush of investors. When everyone else sells, they look for values and buy instead.

When you think of the crush of people on Wall Street shouting "Buy! Buy! Sell!" — you are seeing the Chicken Littles in action. They are concerned with what the market is doing right now. Perma-Bulls are more concerned with what will happen to the market in the next ten years, and they are content to hold or buy stocks that the Chicken Littles are selling. Wall Street needs both types of investors to function, and it is up to you to decide which one you will be.

Each philosophy has its flaws. Chicken Little investors get caught up in the excitement of the buy and sell mentality and make poor decisions. They also pay far more in brokerage and trade fees and in capital gains taxes because they own their stocks less than a year before they sell them. Perma-Bulls, on the other hand, can have a tendency to hold their stock past the point when they should have sold it to make the largest profit. The best philosophy is to strike a wide path through the middle. Avoid getting caught up in short-term market fluctuations, but do not be so attached to your stocks that you refuse to sell when it benefits you.

Timing the Market

Americans may avoid investing in stocks because they are afraid of taking a risk with their money. They are either uninformed, or they do not want to do the research involved. It is easy to get caught up in the Chicken Little mentality and purchase stocks just because you hear or read about them and think they might be a good value.

Buying and selling stocks frequently is done with the intent to time the market and make large gains in a short amount of time. But this type of trading is one of the worst mistakes a new investor can make. For most of us, attempting to time the market is the quickest road to financial ruin.

The key to successful retirement investing is the exact opposite of timing the market. When you decide to invest, consult with a financial advisor, who can help you set up a plan that will meet your retirement goals in the time you have available. Deciding on a plan that will meet all of your financial goals within a specific period of time is not an easy thing to do, and the money you spend to meet with an expert who can look at your unique financial picture will pay dividends that far outweigh the cost of the meeting.

One of the first things you will need to know to begin investing for retirement is that to amass true wealth, you must invest your money for the long haul. This means that before you can begin investing, you have to have enough money in liquid accounts, like checking and savings accounts, to protect yourself in case of an emergency. Stock sales are subject to taxes that vary, depending on how long you have owned the stock. Selling stock you recently purchased incurs a capital gains tax of up to 28 percent. The longer you own the stock before you sell it, the lower the taxes are on the sale, as low as 5 percent in some cases.

The main reason you need to invest over a period of years rather than days or months is that there are years that the stock market will not do so well and years that it will grow. The stock market is subject to all manner of pressures and has natural cycles of highs and lows. After the attacks on the World Trade Center, the stock market took a long time to rebound. If it had been necessary for you to sell your stocks during that period, you would have taken quite a loss. Where the stock market is concerned, persistence is king.

If you are putting money into an IRA account, you will face heavy penalties for pulling it out early, so much so, that using that money for anything except retirement needs to be a last resort. Keep a cushion of money available to you at all times so you do not have to dip into these savings until your plan calls for it. Once your emergency plan is in place, you are ready to being investing. If you can begin investing armed with the knowledge that once you start, your money needs to stay there for years, you are ready to take the next step.

Risk Versus Reward

At the heart of all financial gain lies risk. When a bank lends you money, they take a calculated risk in order to collect interest on the payments. When you invest in the stock market, you also take a calculated risk with your money. It is possible to lose every dollar that you ever put into the stock market. However, barring a massive incident, it is probable that you will come out ahead, and better, for the investment.

The greater the risk you are willing to take with your money, the greater the potential reward. It is why people with bad credit pay higher interest rates. They are more of a risk so the bank asks for more of a reward when lending them money. There are no safe investments — only various degrees of risk.

You have many ways to offset your risk where the stock market is concerned. Investing in professionally managed mutual funds is one option. Index funds, like the S&P 500, are another. These are umbrella funds that allow you to broadly diversify your investments in many companies at once with less risk than investing in a single company. The return is often a nice, steady growth rather than large peaks of profit and valleys of loss. By utilizing these types of funds, you are not tied to the fortunes of a single company, but to sections of the stock market as a whole.

Ignore Uneducated Advice

When you first begin investing, you will be subject to opinions of everyone from your next door neighbor to your golf caddy on exactly where you should invest your hard-earned money. There are so-called experts that scream to the rafters about the next hot pick, the next sure thing, and where this sector or that sector of the market will go in the future.

Ignore such people. You are investing for the long term not the short term. While one section of the market is down, another will be up. If you are properly diversified, your portfolio can withstand these fluctuations with no trouble. Stay away from "hot picks" and individual companies, and watch your investments grow over time.

Be wary of companies who try to draw you in with promises of free information. "Visit our Web site and research every stock available on the market," they cry. Then when you least expect it, you start getting e-mails: "Ten stocks you have to own now," or, "Download this free guide that can double your retirement savings."

These e-mails and downloads will contain just enough truth to help you make a bad decision. They will spend the first four or five paragraphs talking about the benefits of long-term investing, and follow it with: "Invest in this company. It's the next Google/

Berkshire Hathaway / safe bet with virtually no risk."

Then you will get mailings with things like this one: "Our top stock picks have outperformed the market by 28 percent." Never mind that they are basing that conclusion on virtual portfolios, where they just track the stocks rather than investing in them.

Simply stated, you would not buy a used car from the dirtiest, greasiest dealer on the lot. So, do not take stock advice from anyone who screams at you to "Buy now. Buy now." If they profit from your decision to buy, you may lose your investment.

The only way to minimize your investment risk is to make an educated decision based on the company's current management, past performance, and future outlook. This decision requires tedious research with no emotion involved at all. If you are emotional about a stock or the possible profits from one, that is an excellent signal to stop what you are doing and rethink the purchase before you hand over your hard-earned cash.

Research Before You Buy

You would not buy a car or a house blindly, no matter how good a deal you might get on it. The same principle applies to purchasing shares of stock. Research your investments carefully before you put your money into a questionable investment.

I cannot stress enough that if you do not have the time to do this, you are better off hiring an expert to manage your investments for you. You might want to use some combination of expert-controlled investments and personal speculation. You would not ask just anyone to prepare your taxes or work on your car: you would visit someone who was trained and competent in the field. It may not keep you from getting ripped off, but at least it makes that possibility less likely.

It is better to begin with a well-managed mutual fund, with all its associated fees, than to make the mistake of buying stock in a company that goes belly up and takes your savings with it. This is your retirement and your security we are talking about. As you become more familiar with the stock market and how it works, you may want to begin investigating in additional options. Make your IRAs, mutual funds, and your 401(k) accounts the basis for your portfolio, and have them professionally managed if at all possible.

Diversify Your Holdings

The key to a successful stock portfolio is the same as the key to your entire financial portfolio: diversity. General Electric, Johnson & Johnson, and Disney may be wonderful and historically secure companies, but if you hitch your wagon to their star and something happens, you could be left without your retirement.

The best answer is to combine the total picture; have three to six months or more of expenses in a high-yield savings account; invest in low-risk securities like bonds and CDs to help offset your risk; invest in different types of funds to have quick access to stock in many companies instead of just one or two. Invest sparingly in single companies, and only when you have everything else in place. Keep an eye on the fees charged, and take a good look at your bottom line on a regular basis.

Again, depending on your goals and the amount of time you have before retirement, your needs could differ from this recommendation. Paying a financial advisor to look at your specific needs will be worth your money and could prevent you from making mistakes common to new investors.

Rebalance Your Portfolio

Spend time each year visiting your investments and rebalancing the allocation of your assets. It is normal that some of your investments will grow in a year and some will shrink. This is dependent upon the economy, the particular industry, the stock market as a whole, and even the world market. You cannot control it you just have to roll with it. Over the course of the year, you will find that some areas of your portfolio have risen or fallen to the degree that the original balance you intended has been lost.

If you set a yearly date to review your investment, it gives you an opportunity to invest more or less money where you need to in order to keep everything in balance.

Your investment portfolio should consist of a nice mix of cash, stocks, and bonds. Keeping a balance of the three reduces your risk and protects the entire portfolio. For example, if your stocks have had a good year, you may find your total value becoming stock-heavy.

If you allow your stock portfolio to get out of balance with the rest of your investments, you will run the risk of losing a large chunk of money if those same stocks decrease in value. If you keep your portfolio properly balanced, even if the value of your stocks drop, you will still have your cash and bonds to protect yourself if you need them.

A general rule of thumb is to rebalance the money whenever your values are 5 percent or more away from your original intent.

For example, if your portfolio was allocated as follows:

40 percent — stocks

40 percent — bonds

20 percent — cash

And your stocks jumped sharply, you would see your portfolio looking more like this:

50 percent — stocks

35 percent — bonds

15 percent — cash

At that point, you have two options.

1. Sell some of your high-performance stocks or your under performing stocks, and reallocate the money to cash or bonds.

2. Increase your savings in the areas of cash and bonds to match the new growth of your stocks.

So how do you know what percentage of which investments you should have in your portfolio? Spend time thinking about what level of risk you are comfortable with. Putting 40 percent of your money into stocks can offer nice returns, but you are exposing that 40 percent to greater risks. Assuming your cash is in a high-interest savings account it is safe, but often not earning much more than 4 percent interest. However, the savings account is a predictable and reliable 4 percent with little risk involved.

Speaking with your financial advisor is a good place to start if you have questions about asset allocation.

Rebalancing and reallocating your investments is all about reducing your risk. These are essential in protecting your retirement savings and planning for a comfortable retirement.

Dollar Cost Averaging

Dollar cost averaging is the cousin of compound interest. It means that you invest a small amount of money regularly, regardless of whether the stock market is up or down. At first, this might seem contradictory to the age-old adage, "Buy low, sell high." In the end, however, it often works out better for you. Instead of trying to time the market's short-term fluctuations, you invest no matter what the market is doing and pull your money out after ten years or more.

By not worrying about the highs and lows, and committing your money for the long haul, you can often come out on top with little sacrifice. But past performance does not guarantee future results, and you can lose money by investing in the stock market. Again, you have to decide what level of risk is appropriate for you to take with your money. Talk with your financial advisor about your goals.

Investment Companies

Today we have an array of options for getting involved in the stock market. Companies like ShareBuilder (owned by ING Direct) offer ways for you to do the opposite of trying to time the market.

ShareBuilder lets you invest any amount of money, as little as $25 a month, into mutual accounts, index funds, even individual stocks. By investing a small amount of money regularly, you can buy partial shares through ShareBuilder and take advantage of dollar cost averaging.

If you have $1000 or more to begin investing right away, it may be wise to look into investing with well-established companies like Vanguard. ShareBuilder is unique in that it allows people with little investment money the opportunity to maximize every dollar possible by buying partial shares of stock. The hope is that ShareBuilder is paving the way for more companies to reach out to investors with less capital.

If you are approaching retirement, it is vital that you not wait any longer to start building a secure financial foundation. Stocks involve a lot of risk, but they are often the best way to maximize your investment returns. Just be sure to balance the risk with enough stable investments, such as CDs, and professionally managed funds.

There are as many different investment philosophies as there are investors, and it is far beyond the scope of this book to tell you what kind of investor you should be. It is my sincere belief that long-term investing provides the most stable returns and will provide for your retirement far better than having a short-term outlook. However, that is something you are going to have to decide for yourself. The best thing you can do is take the time to do your homework and invest according to what you believe in. Whatever you choose to do, sit down with a qualified financial advisor; that is what they do for a living. The professional advisor can look at your unique circumstances and give you specific advice about how to meet your investment goals.

"I'm retired - goodbye tension,
hello pension!"

Author Unknown

10

Researching Stocks & Choosing a Financial Advisor

How to Research a Potential Investment

Before you invest in a fund or an individual company, take a close look at its past performance, future projections, and current management. I wish I could tell you that it is as simple as waving a magic wand and having all the information in front of you, but it often requires quite a bit of work. Some companies attempt to give stocks their own ratings that suggest whether to buy or sell. As you do your research, take these recommendations with a grain of salt. It is difficult to boil a company's information down to a scale of 1 to 10, and their criteria for doing so may not match yours. You are the only person who can decide if an investment is right for you. That said, there are some excellent and informative Internet sites and publications where you can research prospective stocks for free.

When you have targeted a potential investment, research it on the following Web sites:

- **ShareBuilder** — This Web site allows you to search for the stock symbol by the company name, so it's a good place to begin. Also, they keep track of notable news articles relating to the company. It is worth reading the articles, because they give you clues to the types of challenges the company may be facing. Visit **www.ShareBuilder.com** and click on "Research" to get started. If you do not know the ticker symbol of the stock, click on "Find Symbol" under the "Get a Quote" section. Once you get a quote, you can view the company's listed profile, key statistics including their profit margin, a quick assessment of their management's effectiveness, and more.

- **MorningStar.com** — Click on "Stocks" and enter the ticker symbol in the search box. This site features a large selection of graphs to help you determine a company's profit and loss history and investment trends. You can check it out at **www. MorningStar.com**.

- **Yahoo Finance** — You can view the annual reports of companies for free, although you have to jump through several hoops to do it. This site has a variety of articles to browse that may help you gain additional insight into investing. Visit them at **www.YahooFinance.com**.

- **MSN Money** — This Web site offers most of the information you will need in an easy-to-read, understandable format. Just research the ticker symbol and get a quote. You can view all the information for a company, plus related news stories, editorial articles, and a quick graph showing the stock's average growth in the last ten years. Begin your research at **http://moneycentral.msn.com.**

All of these Web sites are good places to begin researching your potential investments. Use the one that is easiest to navigate and makes the most sense to you, because you are going to find the same information on every site. Check the other sites for additional information once you are finished with the first.

So what do all these facts, figures, articles, and graphs mean? Why do you need to understand them? It is simple. If you have ever bet on a horse or a sports team, chances are you took several things into consideration before you placed your bet. If you were going to bet on a horse, you would judge the horse's past performance, the jockey, the trainer, the horse's general health, and the type of track the horse prefers to run on. If you were going to bet on a sports team, you would want to know how many wins and losses they had for the season, how well the coach has guided the team, the averages of the top players on the team, and whether they were playing at home or away — among other things.

When you get right down to it, you are betting on stocks when you invest. Whether it is a mutual fund or an individual stock, you need to take a close look at everything before you invest.

Betting the Horses: Individual Stocks

Consider individual stocks the "horses" you are researching:

How well has it performed in the past? With horses, it is easy; you get a win/loss number. With stocks, it is easy, too. You look at the individual stock's growth over the last ten or twenty years.

Has the value of the stock consistently risen? If you see steady growth, that is a good sign. If you see large peaks and valleys in the value of a stock over several years, this will bear some investigation. Find out why the value of the stock dropped so drastically in those years.

Drops in stock value can be caused by many things. If the value dropped during a recession, this is normal. If it dropped because the manager made poor business decisions, you will need to understand what happened to cause that drop. Is the company still run by the same manager? How likely it is that they will have a repeat of whatever caused the value to drop?

Who are the "jockey" and "trainers" for the company? You need to take a good look at the company's president and board of directors. A quick Google search on "General Electric's board of directors 2008" is a good place to start, but be sure you are looking at information from reputable Web sites. Confirm the information in two or three places, if possible. This will help you determine how qualified the people running the company are; whether or not they have made controversial decisions in the past; and their overall business philosophy. When you get right down to it, these are the people who decide what to do with the money you invest with them, so you want to be sure that your beliefs about where the business should go align with theirs.

How healthy is your "horse?" What is the current value of the stock you are thinking of investing in? Is it higher or lower than it has been in the past? Does it pay dividends? Has it split recently? Have dividends been cut recently? It's like being allowed to give your horse a physical before the race. A thorough check-up can spot problems before you invest and lose money.

What type of track does this horse prefer to run on? There are two aspects to this when you are talking about stocks. The first depends on why you are buying the stock. Are you purchasing it with the intent to hold it for a short time or a long time?

If you are purchasing a stock, hoping for short-term gains, look for stocks that are undervalued and then keep a close eye on their growth to determine the best time to sell. If you are planning to hold on to them longer, look then for stocks that can go the distance and provide a nice return over many years. The best option for long-term investors is the dollar cost averaging approach. Once you find a company you believe in, purchase the stock regularly, no matter what the short-term cost of the stock is, and hold on to it until you need to sell it as part of your retirement income.

The second aspect of the "track" involves the economy. The stock market is tied to the economy. Some stocks do well in a recession, while others do poorly even in a bull market. Securities like gold and precious metals do well even during recessions. Other stocks, like technology-based companies, tend to be among the first to head south when recession rears its ugly head.

When you are choosing investments, take a good look at what the economy is doing right now and where it may go in the next ten years. For example, as of this writing the financial and housing sectors are trading low because of the recent housing-bubble fiasco. Experts are screaming, "Recession, recession." If your intent is to buy and hold stocks for a long time, you may do the research and believe that now is a good time to invest in the housing and financial sectors of the market. If you have a short-term focus, you will want to stay clear of these investments over the next two to ten years because they will take that long to climb out of the hole they are in.

Whatever you invest in, go into it with the knowledge that it involves taking risks with your money. Investing in individual stocks is accepting the biggest risk of all. Only research and careful investing can help offset that risk. Do not ever take anyone's word that now is the time to buy anything without researching it first.

Betting on Teams: Managed Investment Funds

Managed funds, like mutual funds, index funds, and exchange traded funds, are more like betting on teams of players than individual horses. There are even more factors to examine before you invest, and you will want to take the time to do it thoroughly.

Who is the "coach?" Coaches call the shots; they tell the team which plays to make; and they remove players and send new ones in if necessary. Fund managers do the same thing with stocks. You invest your money with them, and they call the shots. The fund manager decides when to purchase and sell stocks, and keeps the team of stocks (the overall portfolio) balanced for what they hope will be optimal performance.

Before you invest in a fund, be sure that you understand the manager's track record. Has this person guided the fund to success in the past? Has the total value of investments grown during the time that he or she has been the manager? By what percentage have they grown? Has this person worked anywhere else? How were those funds managed, and why did this person leave?

Who are the most valuable players (MVPs)? By this, I mean what are the star players (stocks) in the portfolio? Where is the bulk of the money invested? Are those choices ones you agree with? Researching the individual companies is a smart move. You will not be able to decide when it is time to buy and sell stocks you own in those companies, but you can be sure they are companies you are comfortable having your money invested in.

Is the fund diversified? Every successful sports team is made up of players with different abilities. Some players need to be able to pass and run quickly, while others need to be able to guard the goal. Stock portfolios work the same way. They should include stocks with different objectives. Some of the "players" in the portfolio should be there specifically for gain (scoring points), while the rest need to be there to run defense so that the fund does not lose value in the long run. In sports, you often find teams that excel at offense but lack good defense, and vice versa.

The same is true of managed funds. If you are concerned with quick growth, you can buy into high-risk funds concerned with returning high profits, or you can buy into low-risk funds that are more concerned with defense and keeping your money safe than with growth.

The best teams have an excellent mix of offense and defense, and you will want to start there when you are considering which funds to invest in. You can buy into moderate-risk funds that attempt to keep your money safe and earn a good return on your investments.

You can also consider the option of adding all three types of funds to your portfolio so that you have the opportunity to diversify in a safe way.

How Much Does the Bookie Get?

Let us carry our sports analogy one step further, and consider this. When you place a large bet on a game, you may do it through a bookie who takes a percentage of your winnings. Again, the stock market is the same way. No matter how you choose to invest, someone is going to have their hand in your pie. How much of your pie you let them take is up to you. If you choose to invest in managed funds, read the fine print carefully to see how much the fund is going to charge you to manage your investments. If you are investing without the guidance of a fund manager, make sure you understand how much you will be charged for each trade.

How to Choose a Financial Advisor

If you do not have the time or the inclination to worry about which mutual funds have the lowest fees or which stocks are poised for growth with less risk, it makes sense to consult with someone who does that for a living. You need to look for specific things before you hire an advisor. You need to make sure you get your money's worth. Also, you need to know that the person you hire has your financial goals in mind rather than his or her own.

The smartest person I ever knew once told me, "Smart people do not have to know everything. They just have to know who to ask." You do not need to have all the answers to your financial questions. You just need to find someone qualified to look objectively at your situation, and give you the answers you need. Spending money to meet with a financial advisor could be the best investment you ever make because this person can help you define a clear path to your goals.

When you decide the time is right to meet with a financial advisor, you may have any number of professionals available in your area. Here are tips on how to choose one that will best meet your needs:

Interview several people. Do not hire the first person you speak with just because he or she seems competent. The term "financial planner" can apply to different areas of specialty. Whether it is taxes, investments, estate planning, or another area of the financial realm, you want to choose one whose specialty matches your individual goals.

Are they certified? Several certifications exist, and this person needs to be certified in at least one of the following: Certified Public Accountant (CPA), Certified Financial Planner (CFP), Chartered Financial Consultant (ChFC), or Certified Public Accountant-Personal Financial Specialist (CPA-PFS).

What experience do they have? Look for someone with a verifiable track record and a strong client base.

Find out what they have to offer you. The services they can offer depend on the licenses they hold. If they are not licensed, they cannot sell you insurance, stocks, or mutual funds. You may not want them to sell you anything at all. You may just be looking for advice. Be sure that the planner's qualifications and history match what you need. If you are looking for advice on how to allocate your portfolio, make sure your planner is well versed in current events and an expert in giving investment advice. You should also look for someone with a tax background to help you navigate laws associated with your retirement funds and the buying and selling of securities.

What is their unique approach to financial planning? Every situation is different, and so is every financial advisor. Some will want to take a look at your entire financial picture, while others may prefer to give advice only on specific areas of your portfolio.

How many people will handle your account? It would be best if you could deal with the same person each time you meet instead of a team of people, who may have to spend time reviewing the details of your account each time you walk through the door.

How much do they charge? Be sure that you are clear on the hourly cost, commissions, and fees you will be charged before you set foot in the door. Many advisors will give free initial consultations, but that is not always the case. Call first to find out about a possible fee, and get all agreements in writing as soon as you decide on the person you want as your advisor.

Conflict of interest disclosure. Ask for this in writing prior to signing on with anyone. If this person is receiving kickbacks or bonuses for referrals, he or she may not have your best financial interests at heart. If this person is unwilling to disclose them to you, he or she does not have your financial interests in mind.

Which boards are they regulated by? All registered financial planners are governed by one or more boards that keep negative background information on file. Contact the boards, and check the advisor's background before you take any financial advice.

Request an ADV form. The ADV form is the form your advisor used when he/she registered with the U.S. Securities and Exchange Commission. If this person does not have one, run, do not walk, to the door. This form should contain all their pertinent information, including his or her education and any disciplinary action that has been taken against this person in the last ten years.

To help locate certified professionals in your area, you can contact the National Association of Personal Financial Advisors (NAPFA), the Financial Planning Association (FPA), the American Institute of Certified Public Accountants (AICPA), or the National Association of Enrolled Agents (NAEA).

Take the time to prepare a few things in advance of your first meeting. Take a note pad and pen with you, as well as a completed net worth worksheet (one is included below), a current listing of your income and annual expenses, and a list of your financial goals. Showing up without these things is only going to waste time. If you do not bring these items to the first meeting, chances are you will have to pay this person hourly to review the same paperwork later. Take advantage of the free consultation by being as prepared as possible.

Net Worth Worksheet

Part I - Your Assets

1) Checking and Savings Accounts -

Total all your bank accounts here. Do not include your retirement accounts, but do include your money market accounts, if applicable.

Checking and savings: $ _____

2) Your Home - If you own your home, enter its estimated value here. Do not subtract what you owe on your mortgage yet; just enter what your home would be worth if you sold it today.

Home value: $ _____

3) Rental or Other Properties - List the current estimated value(s).

Other properties: $ _____

Net Worth Worksheet

4) Vehicles - Enter the estimated Kelly Blue Book value of your vehicles here. Include boats, RVs, motorcycles, and so on. To find the value of your vehicles, visit Kelly Blue Book online at **www.KBB.com.**

Vehicle #1 $ _____

Vehicle #2 $ _____

Vehicle #3 $ _____

Vehicle #4 $ _____

5) Jewelry/Gems - Watches, rings, chains, and so on.

Jewelry/gems: $ _____

6) Art and Collectibles - What is the estimated value of your collection?

Art and collectibles: $ _____

7) Electronics - Cameras, computers, printers, and so on. Enter the estimated amount you would get if you were going to sell it today, not what you paid for it.

Electronics: $ _____

8) Other Furniture and Household Items - Be sure to enter what you could sell it for today and not what you paid.

Other household goods: $ _____

9) Retirement Accounts - Do not include the estimated value at the time of retirement, just the value if you were forced to cash them out today (before taxes). If you are married, include the retirement accounts of your spouse.

Account #1 $ _____

Account #2 $ _____

Account #3 $ _____

Account #4 $ _____

Account #5 $ _____

Account #6 $ _____

Total for all retirement accounts:

$ _____

Net Worth Worksheet

11) Mutual Funds - List the total value of your funds.

Mutual funds: $

12) Savings Bonds, CDs, and Other Investments -

Other investments: $ _____

13) Insurance - If your life or other insurance policy has a cash-value option, list it here.

Insurance #1 $ _____

Insurance #2 $ _____

Insurance #3 $ _____

Insurance #4 $ _____

Total cash value for all insurance policies:

$ _____

14) Other - List any other assets not mentioned here.

Other #1 $ _____

Other #2 $ _____

Other #3 $ _____

Total for other assets:

$ _____

15) Now total the entire list of your assets.

Total assets:

$ _____

Part II - Your Liabilities

1) Your mortgage - Enter any amount that you still owe on your mortgage.

Total amount due on your mortgage:

$ _____

2) Second Mortgage - Enter any amount due on a second mortgage.

Net Worth Worksheet

Total amount due on your second mortgage:

$ _____

3) Home Equity Loan - List your home equity loans here.

Total amount due on your home equity loan:

$ _____

4) Car Loans - List your auto or recreational vehicle loans here.

Total due for vehicle #1 $ _____

Total due for vehicle #2 $ _____

Total due for vehicle #3 $ _____

Total due for vehicle #4 $ _____

Total amount owed for all vehicles:

$ _____

5) Personal Loans - List any personal loans you have here.

Personal loan #1 $ _____

Personal loan #2 $ _____

Total for personal loans:

$ _____

6) Other Loans - List any additional loans you have outstanding.

Other loan #1 $ _____

Other loan #2 $ _____

Other loan #3 $ _____

Total for additional loans:

$ _____

7) Credit Cards - List all your credit cards here. List any additional cards on the back.

Card name: _____

Balance on credit card #1 $ _____

Net Worth Worksheet

Card name: _____

Balance on credit card #2 $ _____

Card name: _____

Balance on credit card #3 $ _____

Card name: _____

Balance on credit card #4 $ _____

Card name: _____

Balance on credit card #5 $ _____

Card name: _____

Balance on credit card #6 $ _____

Card name: _____

Balance on credit card #7 $ _____

Card name: _____

Balance on credit card #8 $ _____

Total for all credit cards: $ _____

8) Co-signed Loans - If you co-signed on a loan, you could be called to repay it.

Total responsibility for co-signed loans: $ _____

9) Additional Liabilities - List any additional debt.

Other item #1 $ _____

Other item #2 $ _____

Other item #3 $ _____

Other item #4 $ _____

Other item #5 $ _____

10. Stocks — Enter the approximate amount you would receive if you liquidated your portfolio today.

Stocks: $ _____

Net Worth Worksheet

Total for other liabilities: $ _____

11) Now total the entire list of your liabilities.

Total liabilities:

$ _____

Your net worth equals your assets minus your liabilities.

Total from your asset column: $ _____

Total from your liability column: $ _____

Your net worth equals: $ _____

Section 3

Retirement & You

Introduction

Retirement means different things to each of us. For some it means a chance at a new career or a time of peace with their family. For others, it means endless get-togethers, morning golf games, and a chance to pursue hobbies for which there never seemed to be enough time. Maybe it is rocking on the front porch, lemonade, or finally getting to read the morning paper. Perhaps it is about fewer deadlines and less stress. Is any of this sounding familiar?

These are the positive fantasies many of us have about our retirement. Hiding underneath that happy anticipation is the ever-present fear that our money will run out before we do. This fear can create such stress in our lives that many of us throw up our hands and avoid the topic of retirement altogether.

You are the only one who can decide what your retirement should be. That is why this book was created — to help you design an individual plan to meet your retirement goals.

I have seen experts, television specials, and tent revivals advising that you need a whopping $1,000,000 set aside before you retire. Well, sure, that is great advice. Who would not like to do that? Unfortunately, unless you started saving for retirement at age 25 or you manage your investments like Warren Buffett, chances are you can kiss that golden million goodbye.

So what is the good news for the rest of us? The typical over-age-75 household spent an average of $25,763 in 2004. Even carried out over 25 years, that is far less than the intimidating $1,000,000 figure.

Your expectations for retirement may fall somewhere in between the $25,000 and $1,000,000 mark. You are the only one who knows what you want, and you are the only one who can create the plan for your retirement. No formula or figure created by someone else can tell you how much you will need to live happily in retirement. Only careful planning, constant money management, and smart investing can solve the puzzle for you.

What Is Your Ideal Retirement Age?

One of the most crucial questions pertaining to retirement is "when." How old should you be when you retire?

The real question is, "How old do you want to be when you retire?" How many years away is that happy day? Lack of planning is only going to push that date out farther. If you are nearing your retirement age and do not have a solid plan in place, it is crucial that you start today. It is far better to take action now than to hope it will be all right later.

Here are some important dates:

- You are eligible to file for Social Security at 62 years old. However, if you do, you will receive less than if you waited to file until age 65 or older.

- Anyone born after 1960 can expect their Social Security benefits to be reduced if they choose to file early.

- You can apply for Medicare at age 65.

- You can begin penalty-free withdrawals from your 401k and IRAs at 59 and a half years.

- You must start taking payments from your traditional IRA by 70 and a half years.

- Most places will give you senior discounts between 50 and 60 years old.

The difference between when you want to retire and when you will be able to retire is up to you. We have already discussed ways to cut spending and begin investing. In this section, we are going to focus on retirement itself. We will take a look at ways to supplement your retirement income, what you can expect from Social Security and Medicare, annuity options, and even retiring overseas. Then we are going to put it all together, and help you figure out how much you will need to retire, and where that money is going to come from.

11

Supplemental Income During Retirement

Most people's retirement questions include, "How in the heck am I going to be able to afford it?" and "When can I afford to do it?" Another honest question is, "Do I want to work during my retirement?" Better standards of living and advancements in medical care have caused many of us to revise our picture of retirement.

Not everyone wants to fade quietly into the sunset for 20 or 30 years. Instead, as we feel better, eat better, and exercise more, we wonder how we will fill our days and what we will do with all that time. If you add two or more mortgages and a pile of credit card debt to those questions, a working retirement may begin to look good.

By the time you finish this book, you should know whether a working retirement is for you. If you find that you have to work out of necessity, you will at least know how many more years it will take to reach your retirement goals. That is much better than being afraid you will have to work forever just to get by.

It will be easier if you view retirement as a process or a journey. If you have not saved enough money to retire fully, consider phasing into retirement. Perhaps you are financially secure enough that a full-time job is not required after you retire. You or your spouse could work part-time and gain added financial security if need be. Studies have shown that this makes a much easier transition than retiring "cold turkey." After working all your life, you may find yourself going out of your mind after a month at home.

Retirement often puts a strain on marriage as well, especially if one spouse is retired and the other is not. Being home alone all day may hard to get used to. On the other hand, if you retire together and find yourself home with your spouse 24 hours a day after having a different routine all your married life, an adjustment period can be expected.

Both men and women define themselves through their job — at least in part. Retiring can suddenly mean a loss of identity, a perceived lack of self-worth, and even the cause of depression. Taking a part-time job after, or even before, retiring can help ease this transition, mentally as well as financially.

If you decide to take a part-time job during retirement, you have a multitude of options. The trap is not finding something to fill your days. Retirement, as we most often imagine it, rocking on the front porch with a glass of tea and quietly fading away, is just not cutting it.

Working During Retirement

It is possible that you will be disgruntled and sore after sitting in that rocker for even two days, much less 10 or 20 years. For many people, the question is not if they will work during retirement; it is what job they should take?

The answer is different for everyone. The most interesting proposition is doing something you love. It could be a hobby you have never had time for or something you have wanted to learn and do since you were young. Take what you love and find a way to make money out of that.

In this respect, retirement holds as much opportunity as when you were just starting out in life. If you have worked most of your life in a job that you did not love, retirement can be your chance to explore other, less stressful possibilities.

More retirees are deciding to take the retirement plunge while taking on a part-time job working from home. You may have the option of purchasing rental property or starting a business. The key is to stick with what you know and love. Many options are available to you to supplement your retirement income:

- **Tutoring** — Everyone is good at something. You do not have to be an expert in calculus to tutor someone. If you can read, you can help a child learn. If you are certified to drive a forklift, you could obtain an instructor's certification and train others how to do it. If you are good with computers, you can show others how to use software. If you can sew or bake, you can give lessons. The possibilities are endless. Whatever your skill is, chances are someone else wants to learn it, and would pay you to teach them.

- **Freelance Writing** — A new era is happening in publishing. The Internet has blown the writing profession wide open. If you can write well, this could be a viable second career.

- **Photography** — If you have always been the one who chased your family members around with a camera and dreamed of the perfect lighting, this might be a fun profession for you. Local newspapers, magazines, and even the Internet provide ample places to market your work.

- **Grant Writing** — The government is not throwing money at people or companies, no matter what those ads on TV might lead you to believe. Grant writing is a specialized skill that is in high demand. If you are willing to learn how to do it, companies are looking for your services.

- **Personal Chef** — You can try your hand at cooking for those in need: the elderly, the well-off who do not cook, and those who cannot do it for themselves. You could even audit some cooking classes at the local college for free.

- **Artist** — This is a tough medium to get into and it takes talent. If you think you have what it takes, the Internet allows you to contact galleries halfway around the world or set up your own gallery online.

- **eBay Expert** — These businesses often sound more viable than they are, but if you take the time to learn the ins and the outs, there is money to be made.

- **At-Home Collections Officer** — This is also a trained profession, but it pays well and offers steady work.

- **Private Eye** — If you have ever wanted to know what it takes to be a private investigator (PI), what are you waiting for? Background information is readily available online for a low cost.

- **Medical Billing** — This is also a trained profession. You may find some companies willing to train you to do it, but you will probably have to enroll in classes at a community college or vocational school to learn all you need to know. Once you understand the billing codes, you can command a decent wage per hour.

The best way to merge into a second career based on a hobby is to begin well before retirement. You will be better off if you can have a steady second income already flowing before you take the next step into retirement. If you plan to work for someone else, try picking up a few hours on the weekends or evenings to see if it is a good fit.

Networking is still one of the best ways to get a job today. Word of mouth is your friend. If you plan to work after retirement, let everyone know as soon as possible. You might be surprised at the offers you receive if you put the word out early.

Use your existing connections at work to help you get on track before you take the plunge. It is easier to hear about opportunities when you still see your coworkers every day than to try and take advantage of the connection months later when you are not at the top of their thoughts.

If you plan to start your own business, begin your research long before you need to depend on the income. Starting a business is not as easy as it sounds. Legal and tax hurdles must be overcome before your business can get off the ground.

Also, small businesses often require a sizeable initial investment. No matter what you choose to do, you will need start-up money. If you start before retirement, it will give you time to spread that cost out and still have the security of your normal income. You can also maximize your current contacts and get as much referral business as possible prior to doing it full-time.

The key with any profession, especially ones you plan to do from home, is to get them established before you hope to retire. In other words, do not quit your day job before you have something stable to fall back on.

Using Rental Properties for Additional Income

Purchasing real estate is an investment, just like any other. It involves risk, risk that you will not be able to sell or rent the building or land you purchased, and the risk of being forced to make the payments yourself. It often forces you to become a debtor by taking on a loan for another property when you may not have yours paid off yet.

If you tie the financing for your new property to the home you are living in, you run the risk of losing your home if something happens. Tax laws and implications must be dealt with, as well as maintenance of the new property and the search for renters. With all that to deal with, you may wonder, "Why bother?" The answer to that is simple. With hard work, research, and careful maintenance, there is the possibility of earning a regular income that will be enough to supplement your retirement.

With the recent bust of the real estate market, there are a few things to consider. As of this writing, lenders are being careful about who they lend money to. Unless you have excellent credit, you may find it difficult to get a loan for an additional property. However, with the crush of people caught in the adjustable rate mortgage (ARM) trap, foreclosed homes are becoming common. Just like value stocks, foreclosed homes can offer a nice way to get a larger return for less initial investment.

In purchasing rental property, you will pay all the same fees that you paid when you purchased the house you are currently living in. You will have to deal with refinancing and finding reliable tenants also. Then there are tax issues involved with owning a rental property.

You will have to contend with regular maintenance on a property you are not living in. It can be hard at times to deal with unexpected maintenance problems in our own home. When the roof leaks, the gutters are torn off in a storm, or the water heater fails, you will be the one who is responsible for the repair in that rental property. That means you are going to have to set aside a separate savings account for your rental property and have the discipline to pay into it regularly. Otherwise, you may be forced to borrow money on credit or against the value of your own home to fix the rental problem.

It is beyond the scope of this book to cover all the ins and outs of the real estate market. Just be aware that it is a viable way for you to earn additional retirement income, as long as you manage it like any other investment.

If you would like more information about how to purchase or rent homes for profit, check out these books. They should all be available from Amazon.com, your local bookstore, or your library.

- *Retire on the House: Using Real Estate to Secure Your Retirement,* by Gillette Edmunds and James Keene

- *Building Real Estate Wealth in a Changing Market: Reap Large Profits from Bargain Purchases in Any Economy,* by John W. Schaub

- *Building Wealth One House at a Time: Making It Big on Little Deals,* by John W. Schaub

- *The Part-Time Real Estate Investor: How to Generate Huge Profits While Keeping Your Day Job,* by Dan W. Blacharski

Annuities

Annuities are presented here because they offer an additional way to supplement your retirement income. They are not the right choice for everyone, but this section should help you decide if they are an option you want to consider.

Annuities are insurance policies designed to help you supplement your retirement income. They are sold by life insurance companies as well as financial brokers.

How do they work?

Annuities work much like a normal insurance policy in that you pay the company a premium each month for a number of years. Unlike a typical insurance policy, you have the option of purchasing an annuity with a one-time, lump-sum payment. This is a good option if you must withdraw your 401(k) money or your IRA money but you do not yet want to tap into it. You can roll the money over into an annuity and defer the taxes until you are ready to start taking payments from.

The biggest advantage of an annuity is that your money grows tax-deferred until you are ready to withdraw it, just like your other primary retirement accounts. The money you invest in an annuity will either earn a set rate of interest decided at the time of purchase or earn a variable rate of interest, depending on which stocks or other securities the money is invested in.

The date that you choose to access the funds is known as the maturity date for the annuity. If you choose an early annuity date and withdraw funds before you reach the age of 59 and a half, you will still have to pay the IRS a penalty of 10 percent for early withdrawal.

Here are the four most common types of annuities.

1. **A single-premium immediate annuity** – You purchase this type of annuity with a lump-sum payment, and you begin making withdrawals within one month of purchase. You receive regular amounts of money for a length of time that you and your insurance company agree upon. How much money you will be paid each month depends on how long you want your money to last. Your investments will grow at a set interest rate that is decided by the issuing company each year.

2. **A single-premium deferred annuity** – This is the same as a single-premium immediate annuity, except you wait to begin receiving payments. It is purchased with a lump-sum payment and earns a regular, set rate of interest.

3. **An annual premium-deferred annuity** — With this type of annuity, you send your insurance company money at regular intervals instead of in one lump sum. You can pay the premiums monthly, quarterly, or yearly. Your money will earn a set rate of interest, and your withdrawals are deferred until you are ready to access your funds in retirement.

4. **Variable annuity** — This type of annuity earns a variable rate of interest and involves investing your money in securities such as stocks and bonds. You can purchase them either with a lump-sum payment or by making regular monthly payments to your insurance company. The amount you will have available to begin withdrawing at retirement depends on how well your investments performed. You decide what your money is invested in, and you can invest as aggressively or moderately as you want.

A word of warning: It is unwise to pull money out of your other tax-deferred accounts in order to purchase an annuity. The only time you would use these accounts to fund an annuity is if you must begin taking payments out of your 401(k) or traditional IRA by law, yet you do not want to use the money.

Otherwise, the best bet is to make regular monthly or quarterly payments to your insurance company to purchase the annuity. If you do, it will be additional retirement income rather than just shuffling the same money around from one tax-deferred account to another.

Another caution: Be careful when choosing the company through which you purchase your annuity. Treat this investment as if you were purchasing stock in an individual company, and in a sense you are. If you want your annuity to last throughout your retirement, you need to choose a company that is going to be around as long as you are.

"Retirement means no pressure, no stress, no heartache... unless you play golf."

Gene Perret

12

Social Security, Medicare, & Insurance

Social Security and Medicare are large question marks for most of us when we think about retirement. Will Social Security still be around when it is time for me to start collecting it? How much will I receive? How long will they pay me? Will it be enough to help me supplement my income?

The important thing to remember is that Social Security and Medicare were never designed to be your only income in retirement. With their decidedly shaky future, it is best not to count on them at all if your retirement date is ten or more years away. Changes need to be made to both programs for them to survive and continue paying out beyond that point.

Why are Social Security and Medicare going under? Boiled down to the simplest terms, the fund managers have been short-sighted. Approximately 77 million Baby Boomers have retired and are collecting Social Security and Medicare. As more of this generation retires more people than ever before will be drawing funds and fewer people will be paying into them.

We all know what happens when your bills exceed your income; you are forced to go into debt. The government is going to be forced to assume trillions of dollars of debt that they have not planned for. The most likely result is that they will attempt to restructure the programs, slash benefits, raise taxes, and keep Social Security and Medicare limping along — at least for a while.

Social Security

Social Security is a government pension program designed to supplement your retirement income by taking money out of your check each time you get paid and adding it to the fund. When you retire, you can begin collecting money from the fund for the rest of your life. The only problem is that the fund has no reserves and it is about to have to write a large check to our retiring seniors. The check is going to bounce throughout Washington, D.C. and every aspect of the federal budget, and all the way down to you and me in the form of increased taxes.

There is a common misconception that the funds you have been paying into Social Security via your payroll check are held in reserve and perhaps earning interest for you. The nasty truth is that the money deducted from your check is coming in and going out to a current retiree in the same month, if not the same day.

The following information comes from our government's own facts via Social Security Online. See **www.SSA.gov** for more information.

Currently, Social Security is taking in more than it is paying out, so it is doing a little better than Medicare.

The bad news is that by 2017, so many people will have retired, there will no longer be enough income to support the needed outflow. At that point, the program will be forced to dip into its trust reserves in order to meet the demands of nearly 77 million retirees.

If no changes are made, the projected year for the collapse of our Social Security system is 2041.

The system will attempt to adapt and overcome the issues. But it will meet with the same problems plaguing Medicare because more people will be collecting benefits than there are paying into the system.

Probable changes to Social Security include a higher age to qualify, reduced benefits, and higher payroll taxes. Social Security payroll taxes already have increased 20 times throughout the life of the program. The most dire doom-and-gloomers predict that taxes would have to increase as much as 50 percent in order to cover the projected cost of the Baby Boomers' retirements.

If you are going to be able to collect Social Security soon, that is wonderful. Take advantage of it. Just like Medicare, you can consider it a nice addition to your retirement income, but not the meat and potatoes of it.

For those retiring soon, Social Security may still be a viable source of retirement income. Let us take a look at what you can expect when you get ready to apply for it.

Current Benefits and Restrictions of Social Security

The earliest you can begin to collect Social Security benefits is age 62. This is considered early retirement, and will result in your being paid less than if you had waited a few years. As far as Social Security is concerned, full retirement age is between 65 and 67 years old, depending on your date of birth.

If you choose to collect your benefits early, you will only receive about 80 percent of your estimated benefits over time. The best choice is to wait until you are 65 to apply for benefits so that you can collect the full amount. In this respect, it is just like withdrawing from your IRA or 401(k) account early. It is best to wait if you want to avoid taking that penalty.

If you wait until you reach your full retirement age to apply for benefits, you will be paid 100 percent of what is owed to you each month for as long as the program lasts or until your death.

Full Retirement Age

Here is a current list of what the Social Security Administration considers "full retirement age." It varies from 65 to 67, based on your birthday, and that number is likely to be moved higher in the future.

Retirement Ages	
If you were born between:	Your full retirement age is:
1. January 1, 1938 or earlier	1. 65
2. January 2, 1938 — January 1, 1939	2. 65 and 2 months
3. January 2, 1939 — January 1, 1940	3. 65 and 4 months
4. January 2, 1940 — January 1, 1941	4. 65 and 6 months
5. January 2, 1941 — January 1, 1942	5. 65 and 8 months
6. January 2, 1942 — January 1, 1943	6. 65 and 10 months

Retirement Ages	
7.	January 2, 1943 — January 1, 1955	66
8.	January 2, 1955 — January 1, 1956	66 and 2 months
9.	January 2, 1956 — January 1, 1957	66 and 4 months
10.	January 2, 1957 — January 1, 1958	66 and 6 months
11.	January 2, 1958 — January 1, 1959	66 and 8 months
12.	January 2, 1959 — January 1, 1960	66 and 10 months
13.	January 2, 1960 or later	67

So How Much Will You Collect from Social Security?

Current benefit projections for withdrawing at your full retirement age (not early) are as follows:

- "Low income" workers who make $11,554 a year or less can expect to collect around 56 percent of their pre-retirement income.

- "Average income" workers who earn around $25,676 a year will collect around 42 percent of their pre-retirement income.

- "High income" workers earning $62,700 a year or more can expect to get only about 28 percent of their pre-retirement income.

It is important to note that pension payments, annuities, and the interest or dividends from your savings and investment accounts are not considered "earnings" as far as Social Security is concerned. You may still have to pay income taxes on these earnings, but you will not have to pay into Social Security on them.

Social Security Benefits

Your Social Security benefits will be calculated based on your average lifetime earnings. The Social Security Administration defines "lifetime earnings" as the 35 years of your life in which you earned the most money. If you did not work for a total of 35 years, years counting as "zero income" will be added in until they reach 35 working years. Your earnings are then adjusted to reflect changes in the "average wage" during the years you worked. Since there are several rather ambiguous steps to figuring out how much you will collect in benefits from Social Security, it is best to use their calculator online if you want the most accurate results.

The calculator is located at **http://www.ssa.gov/retire2/ AnypiaApplet.html.**

A more detailed calculator is available for you to download at **http://www.ssa.gov/OACT/anypia/anypia.html.**

The third and final way to estimate your Social Security benefits is by using the free statement they issue you every year. If you lost or never received your statement this year, you can request another one at **http://secure.ssa.gov/apps6z/isss/main.html.**

Please be aware that Web site addresses can change over time. If your copy of this book is old, these links may not work. You can always find the information by starting at the Social Security Administration's home page at **www.SSA.gov.**

If you continue to work after you start receiving Social Security payments, you will have to continue to pay Social Security taxes on those earnings.

Applying for Social Security

You can now apply for your Social Security benefits online at **www.SocialSecurity.gov**. Also, you can arrange to apply via telephone by calling 1-800-772-1213 or by visiting your local Social Security office. If you are deaf or hard of hearing, you can use the available text telephone (TTY) telephone number at 1-800-325-0778.

If you want your benefits to begin with your full retirement age, currently 65 to 67, depending on when you were born, you can apply up to four months before you want your benefits to begin. The Social Security Administration encourages you to apply at least three months before you intend to start collecting benefits so that they have time to set up your account.

When you get ready to apply, you will need:

- Your Social Security number

- An original birth certificate (or a certified copy)

- The W-2 forms or your self-employment tax return from the previous year

- If you were not born in the United States, you will need proof of U.S. citizenship or lawful alien status

- The name of your bank, the account number, and routing

number so that your payments can be directly deposited into your account

All these documents must be originals or certified copies. You can either mail them or bring them into the Social Security office that is closest to you. If you plan to mail these documents, it is wise to pay for several copies in case something gets lost in the mail. Ordering only one copy of your birth certificate and then having it get lost between the post office and the Social Security Administration could delay your benefits. Have several copies waiting so that there will be no delay if something happens.

If you need to order copies of your birth certificate, you can visit the National Center for Health Statistics online. You will want to use Google and search the terms "National Center for Health Statistics Birth Certificate" because the Internet address is long and complicated. This Web site will give you the contact information for the Health Statistics office in each state. Contact them to request your copies.

Cost-of-living increases are factored into your benefits, and this may help some, but sadly, even if Social Security does manage to pay you what you are owed, it will be far less than you are used to living on.

It is essential that you develop other types of accounts that will supplement your retirement. Counting on what amounts to a pittance, with no guarantee of even getting that much from the government, is a poor way to plan your future. It would be best to look at Social Security as a wonderful thing if it happens and not as a lifeline to secure your retirement. Do not plan on Social Security at all. Make other plans now, while you have the chance, so that you do not have to rely on the government to support you in your old age.

Medicare

Medicare is a government-sponsored healthcare program for people age 65 and over, as well as for people with disabilities. It is available regardless of your income level. Unfortunately, it is in no better shape than Social Security.

The National Bipartisan Commission on the Future of Medicare gives us these facts.

The Balanced Budget Act (circa 1997) protected the trust fund for exactly ten years. If no changes are made, it will be bankrupt in 2008.

Approximately 77 million Baby Boomers are expected to enroll in Medicare by the year 2011. As more people retire, fewer workers than ever will be available to fund the Medicare system.

Once Medicare is bankrupt, it will begin to use funds intended for other programs. By 2030, the commission estimates that Medicare costs will run between $2.2 and $3 trillion dollars.

There is no way for the federal budget to absorb that amount yearly. Trying to save the system will lead to higher taxes, raising the qualification age, higher out-of-pocket expenses, limited coverage, or exempting certain conditions.

Do you see where this is going? The only sane conclusion is to avoid depending on Medicare. It is not a fit foundation for your future health concerns. Consider it more like the "icing on the cake of retirement." If you manage to get benefits for a while, that is wonderful, but don't count on it for a long-term solution.

Current Benefits and Restrictions of Medicare

Currently, to qualify for Medicare you must be a U.S. citizen age 65 or older, or a legal resident of the United States for at least five years, and also age 65 or older. You or your spouse must have worked at least ten years in a job that had Medicare coverage. Exemptions to the 65-or-older rule include:

- You have a disability and have been receiving Social Security Disability Insurance (SSDI) for at least 24 months.

- You get continuing dialysis for permanent kidney failure or need a kidney transplant.

- You have amyotrophic lateral sclerosis (ALS, also known as Lou Gehrig's disease).

Applying for Medicare

You are required to apply for Medicare three months before your 65th birthday, or you can wait for the next general enrollment period after your birthday. The first three months before your 65th birthday are considered the start of your "seven-month initial enrollment period." This is important because you cannot be turned down during this time. If you wait until your initial enrollment time has passed, you could be forced to pay a higher rate for certain plans or be denied access to certain plans based on your current health condition.

If you want to apply for Medicare and Social Security at the same time, you can do so online by visiting **www.SSA.gov**, by calling 1-800-772-1213, or by visiting your local Social Security office.

If you want to apply for Medicare, but do not want to start receiving your Social Security benefits yet, you must call 1-800-772-1213 to make an appointment or visit your local Social Security office.

In order to apply for Medicare, you will need:

- Your birth certificate

- Your Social Security card

- Your driver's license

- Proof of other insurance, if you have any

Medicare's Many Plans

This section is designed only to cover the basics of each plan so that you may begin preparing for retirement. Individual plan premiums will likely increase between now and when you retire, but it will at least give you a ballpark figure to start with when considering your monthly expenses after retirement.

Medicare Part A

Medicare Part A is designed to cover:

- An in-patient stay in a hospital

- Critical care at hospitals

- Skilled nursing facilities (this does not include custodial or long-term care facilities)

- Hospice

- Qualifying home healthcare

If you are age 65 or older and qualify for Social Security, there is no cost for enrolling in Medicare Part A.

If you are under 65 and have a disability, there is no cost to enroll in Medicare Part A, as long as you have been collecting Social Security benefits for at least 24 months.

Medicare Part B

Medicare Part B is more comprehensive than Part A, but it also comes at a price. It is designed to help you pay for doctors' visits, outpatient hospital care, and other medical services that do not require hospitalization, including:

- Regular physician services (your normal doctor visits)

- X-rays and diagnostic lab tests

- Ambulance fees

- Physical therapy

- Occupational and speech therapy

- Rural health clinic visits

- Dialysis supplies and services

- Qualifying vaccines

- Mammograms and Pap smears

- Diabetes screenings

- Colon and prostate cancer screenings

This is not a comprehensive list, and what is covered may change between now and the time you retire. Be certain that you read and understand all the documentation you are given when you apply for Medicare. Which plan you choose to apply for will depend on the unique state of your health. The only way to choose the best plan for your situation is to read everything carefully and make an informed decision.

Currently, Medicare Part B does not cover physicals, hearing aids, eye exams, or most dental services.

How Medicare Part B Works

When you elect to enroll in Medicare Part B, you will have to meet a yearly deductible before they will begin paying benefits. In 2007, the annual deductible requirement was $137. This deductible will most likely increase in the future. After you meet the annual deductible, Medicare will pay 80 percent of the bills for qualified services. The other 20 percent is your responsibility; 100 percent of non-qualified services will be your responsibility as well.

The Cost of Medicare Part B

Enrolling in Medicare Part B is optional, and the premium you pay for the service is based on your income.

Individuals with annual incomes under $80,000 and married couples with annual incomes under $160,000 in 2007 will pay a monthly premium of $93.50. This money is deducted from your Social Security check before it is deposited into your bank account each month.

If you earn more than $80,000 a year, your premiums would currently look like this:

- Individuals with annual incomes between $80,000 and $100,000 and married couples with annual incomes between $160,000 and $200,000 in 2007 will pay a monthly premium of $106

- Individuals with annual incomes between $100,000 and $150,000 and married couples with annual incomes between $200,000 and $300,000 in 2007 will pay a monthly premium of $124.70

- Individuals with annual incomes between $150,000 and $200,000 and married couples with annual incomes between $300,000 and $400,000 in 2007 will pay a monthly premium of $143.40

- Individuals with annual incomes of $200,000 or more and married couples with annual incomes of $400,000 or more in 2007 will pay a monthly premium of $162.10

Medigap Insurance Plans

Medigap insurance is designed to protect you against some common "gaps" in your coverage if you participate in either the Medicare Part A or B plan. If you are eligible to participate in Medicaid, you do not need to apply for Medigap insurance. As long as you apply for Medigap insurance within the first six months of being eligible, you cannot be turned down. You must be 65 or older to qualify.

Currently, 12 different Medigap policies are available for you to purchase, and they are labeled A through L. If you are considering purchasing Medigap insurance, treat it just as you would any other insurance policy. Start a year or so before you retire, and review one plan a month in detail if necessary. Premiums and deductibles vary from one plan to the next, depending on which company you purchased the insurance plan from.

Medicare Advantage – Part C

Medicare Advantage offers you the option of receiving your healthcare through private insurance plans. The following information lists the varieties of insurance plans offered.

Coordinated Care Plans – These include health maintenance organizations (HMOs), preferred provider plans (PPOs), and other network plans. In 2006, Medicare began offering regional PPO plans. Some of the coordinated care plans apply only to people in specific situations, like people receiving both Medicare and Medicaid.

If you choose to participate in a coordinated care plan, you will have to choose a qualifying physician or Medicare will not pay for your services. If you need to see a specialist for any reason, you must obtain a referral from your approved physician. All Medicare Advantage plans encompass all the benefits of Parts A and B. Additional coverage is offered, but will pay more for it.

Private Fee-for-Service Plans (PFFS) — Private fee-for-service plans are not restricted to an in-network physician, and the amount that Medicare pays for each service is calculated based on the individual service provided. Private fee-for-service plans cost more because there are more choices in your care options.

The Centers for Medicare & Medicaid Services (CMS) are required to provide you with a detailed explanation of the Medicare and Medicaid plans. You can read about these plans in their publication, *The CMS Medicare Handbook*. To order it, call 1-800-Medicare, or order it online at **www.Medicare.gov**.

The Cost of Medicare Advantage

Unfortunately, the cost of purchasing Medicare Advantage cannot be boiled down as easily as the cost for participating in Medicare Parts A and B. If you wish to be covered under Medicare Advantage, the cost will depend upon the plan you choose to participate in. Expect additional costs for any services you receive that are over and above the premiums for participating in the plan itself.

Medicare Part D

Medicare Part D is prescription drug coverage provided by private companies that are approved by Medicare.

Part D coverage is not automatically provided with Medicare Parts A and B, but some Medicare Advantage plans may include it. View the specifics of the individual Advantage plan to find out if you will need to enroll in Medicare Part D as well.

It is best to enroll for Medicare Part D when you apply for your other Medicare benefits. If you do not do it at that time, you may enroll annually between November 15 and December 31.

Medicare Part D plans are categorized by the area in which you live. You must choose a plan that serves your area.

Several Part D plans should be available in your area, and there is no strict list of prescriptions they are required to pay for. Review each plan carefully, and be sure that any prescriptions you are currently taking are included in the plan you purchase. You will have a yearly deductible and a co-payment amount based on the plan you choose.

The Cost of Medicare Part D Coverage

Like Medicare Advantage, there are too many coverage options to quote a specific out-of-pocket cost. How much Medicare Part D coverage costs will depend on the plan you choose. Read the fine print carefully to be sure that your prescriptions are covered, what your deductible will be, what the monthly enrollment fee will be, and how much your prescription co-payment will cost.

If you are unable to meet the required deductibles, co-payments, and enrollment fees during retirement, there are plans in place to help you keep the cost of your prescription drugs down. You will have to apply and qualify for them. You can find out more information on low-income Part D exemptions by calling 1-800-Medicare or online at **www.Medicare.gov.**

If you would like more information on Medicare's individual plans, visit these Web sites online: **www.Medicare.gov** or **www.MedicareAdvocacy.org.**

Medicaid

Medicaid is a government assistance program designed to help low-income individuals pay for all or part of their medical care. Eligibility for Medicaid does not depend on your age, it depends on your income and circumstances. Low income alone does not qualify you for Medicaid. You must fit into one of the eligible "groups" of covered circumstances.

Whether you will be eligible for Medicaid is decided at the state level rather than on federal requirements. Different states may have different requirements for eligibility. In all cases, you must be considered at or barely above the federal poverty level to qualify.

Common covered groups of people include:

- Pregnant women

- Children whose families meet the income restrictions

- People receiving supplemental social security income

- Blind or disabled persons.

If you qualify for Medicaid, you may be able to receive free treatment. However, there are some restrictions. Depending on your income and individual situation, you may be required to make a co-payment for certain services.

For more information on Medicaid, visit the Centers for Medicare and Medicaid Services' Web site at **www.cms.hhs.gov.**

Private Health Insurance

With all the problems facing Social Security and Medicare, the logical first step is to pay for, and depend on, private insurance. Those lucky enough to retire with insurance funded by their employers will have a leg up. Everyone else will have to consider throwing their hat into the private insurance arena.

This is the last of the terrible news. Although private insurance companies are currently experiencing a period of growth, they are not growing as fast as they need to grow. Insurance coverage is expensive, even when part of the cost is offset by your employer, and it is getting more so every day. Truly private insurance — as in, not sponsored by your employer — is even more expensive, and it often has a long list of qualifications. Personal dental and vision policies do not yet exist. Price and discount clubs are the only current options for those with no employer-sponsored insurance.

Something must change, and it is likely that as the security of Medicare goes out the window, the demand for private insurance will increase. Increased demand will cause increased competition and increased supply. More insurance companies will want to capitalize on the demand for private insurance policies.

Because of the demand and more competition, private insurance will most likely fall to a reasonable rate. As more people pay for it, the rates should go down for everyone. How long this will take is anyone's guess.

A few companies currently offer private insurance policies to individuals. For more information on their available plans, visit these Web sites:

- **eHealthInsurance.com** — This Web site searches over 160 insurance providers and gives price quotes on the plans they offer. Visit them online at **www.ehealthinsurance.com**.

- **Anthem (Blue Cross Blue Shield)** — This company offers several types of private insurance policies for individuals and families. Visit them online at **www.Anthem.com**.

- **Aetna** — They also offer individual family insurance plans that you can purchase privately. Visit them online at **http://www.aetna.com**.

Insurance during retirement is essential. You are more likely to have health problems once you reach the age of retirement than at any other time in your life. It will take a effort to research all your options, but the worst thing you can do is leave yourself unprepared. At least take the time to research private insurance policies. Even if you do not need them right away, it will arm you with the projected cost that you will have to absorb during your retirement years.

13

Unexpected Options – Retiring Overseas & More

Retiring Overseas

Choosing whether or not to retire overseas can be one of the most exciting and difficult choices you will ever make. The benefits are clear. The cost of living is so much lower in many places that you can live better abroad than in the United States. Healthcare in some countries is comparable, and many countries court retiring seniors by offering special tax exemptions and incentives.

The negatives are obvious, too. You will be farther away from your extended family and far from the life you have always known.

For some people, a clear break from their old habits during retirement is be a good thing. It is a fresh start, an opportunity to begin the next phase of their life with an adventure; an adventure that promises prosperity and comfort in an exotic locale; an adventure with the wind in their hair and the sand under their feet that sounds promising – even exciting.

But before you get swept up in the idea of retiring to a far-away, magical land where you can live like royalty on a modest income, take a closer look at some of the benefits and detriments about living overseas.

What About Your Family?

If you are close to your extended family, moving abroad may be the toughest decision you will ever make. One bit of wisdom may help; if the situation were reversed and it was your children who wanted to move overseas, would you try to change their minds?

In the end this decision is up to you and your spouse if you are married. It is not about your family: your sisters and brothers, children, or grandchildren. When you get right down to it, it is about being able to have an extraordinary quality of life just by moving to a new location.

It may help to make a pro and con list, and give a lot of thought to it. You should be secure in your decision before you bring the topic up to your extended family. Everyone will have an opinion, but no one else will be retiring in your shoes. They will not sit awake and night and wonder, "What if we had moved overseas like we wanted to? Would things be different now?"

If you think that retiring overseas might be an option for you, keep it private, do your research, and vacation in your potential future country as often as possible to be sure it is a good fit. Once you have all your facts worked out — your living expenses here and there, and your real reasons for leaving — it will be time to invite the opinions from others to the table.

You and your extended family may have the same concerns about how you deal with the time and distance? How you remain a part of your extended family while out of the country? With that in mind, here are a few ideas for staying close to your family even if you move far away.

Keep in Touch Regularly

If you can get a reliable Internet connection in your country of choice, you have many options. You can use a telephone service like Vonage to make long distance calls. It works by using your Internet as your phone line and allows you to make long distance calls at a fraction of the traditional prices. You can invest in good Webcam software that will allow you to see and talk to your family any time. Basic Web cameras are now as low as $30 at Wal-Mart. Schedule daily or weekly times to talk to your extended family and keep up with their lives.

With the advent of digital photos, sharing pictures is as easy as uploading them to your computer and hitting "Send." You can receive photos of your grandchildren and extended family any time, and you can send photos to them.

Never underestimate the power of a handwritten note or card. Taking the time once a month to sit down and write to your family will keep you closer than you can ever imagine.

When you combine the phone calls, regular video sessions with a Web camera, and handwritten notes, you may have more contact than many families who live close together. None of this can replace being there with your family, but it helps.

How to Travel Like a Pro

There will always be times when you need to be with your family. It may be birthdays, holidays, or even an emergency. No matter how far away you move, chances are you will want to see them as often as possible. There are several ways to save money when you travel. All require some planning, but they can cut your expenses drastically.

Become familiar with Sidestep.com. This is an online search engine for flights, hotels, and rental cars. They search all the main airlines and rental agencies at once and return the results on one screen. It is a way to compare all the top discount offers at one time. This can help you book your trip either well in advance or on a moment's notice and still save money. The further ahead you book your flight, the cheaper it often is.

If you use credit cards, consider getting one that offers frequent flier rewards. After all you are paying all that interest — why not get a free flight once in a while? Some credit cards offer excellent rewards programs, and blackout dates and restrictions on flights are not as common as popular commercials would have you believe. Read your policy carefully and call customer service if you need to make sure that your country is included in your credit card's reward policy.

Purchase traveler's insurance, and learn to travel light. This will help protect you from the consequences of layovers and lost luggage. In some cases traveler's insurance offers emergency medical benefits. You can never be too protected when you travel, because many decisions will be out of your hands. For instance, you have no say over your departure or arrival times. Even if your flight is booked to depart at a certain time, we all know that is more like an estimate than a fact. Be sure to arrive early enough to make it through customs, and bring as little as possible with you. You will never have to replace what you do not bring.

Ask for a discount on airfare. Most companies have discount policies, but they are not going to chase you down and offer them to you. Do not be afraid to ask because you can get some excellent deals that way — especially if you travel often.

Financial Considerations for Retirement Overseas

Choosing to retire overseas is a huge financial undertaking. It will involve the sale of your current home or finding renters to live in it. It will involve physically moving everything that you own to a new location, finding a new home, and obtaining financing for it. It will also involve transportation costs if you need to travel back and forth several times before you are settled plus assorted fees for passports, vaccinations, and more.

It is easy to be intimidated with everything that is involved in this type of move. The key is to start planning as early as possible; you can do things like open accounts at local banks well in advance to ease the transfer of your money.

Become familiar with certain important tax and income laws. For example, if you remain a U.S. citizen, you will still have to pay taxes no matter where you move. You need to have an accountant or attorney walk you through the United States tax laws for expatriates. You also will have to contact a local accountant who can walk you through your new country's tax laws. The United

States has treaties with certain countries to help you avoid double taxation, but not all countries are included.

More importantly if you are a United States citizen, you can live in most foreign countries, and it will not affect your eligibility for Social Security. But you will not be eligible for Medicare, unless you choose to live in a U.S. territory like Guam or the Virgin Islands.

It is also essential that you update your will and living will to reflect your new country's laws, especially if you purchase property there.

Vacation and Rent First

If you are seriously considering retiring overseas, travel there and vacation in your country of choice as much as possible before taking the leap. When you finally do retire and prepare to move, it is often smarter to rent a home first in your new city.

There are always nuances of a city that you cannot get to know until you live there. Choosing to rent a home first will allow you to understand the neighborhood and community without being locked into a location. This has three advantages.

- It gives you a place to live while the sale of your own house is being finalized. Then you can take the money from that transaction and apply it to the house of your choice in your new country.

- When you move, you may find the neighborhood does not meet with your expectations. By choosing to rent, you are free to move and research surrounding neighborhoods until you find one that you like.

• If you move, and are terribly homesick, you will not have to sell a your new home in order to move back.

The Top Places to Retire Overseas

With all the attendant problems in retiring overseas, why would anyone do it? Cost of living is often the number one answer. In certain countries, the cost of living is so much lower than in the United States that people can experience true wealth on the same amount of money they have always had — or less.

Let us take a look at some of the most recommended places outside of the United States for retirees.

Mexico

Mexico is still the number one recommended place to retire overseas. In different parts of Mexico, you can find everything from bustling cities full of cultural enthusiasm and entertainment to quiet little houses on the beach where you can relax and let your stress slide away.

Mexico's currency is the peso. One U.S. dollar equals about one peso with the dollar being slightly greater in value. The rate is subject to change, however, so check with your bank for the current exchange rate.

Here are some of the most common retirement destinations in Mexico.

Lake Chapala and Ajijic

Lake Chapala is located about 35 minutes south of Guadalajara and currently supports an active community of retired Americans and well-to-do Mexican natives. There are three main towns in Lake Chapala: Chapala, Ajijic, and Jocotepec. They feature quaint outlying villages and clubs that circle the lake. There is an active local culture, and the area is filled with shops, handcrafted goods, plays, restaurants, golf courses, and more.

Lake Chapala is Mexico's largest lake, and water sports are particular favorites of the residents. It is a little bit of civilization that still clings to a quiet Mexican atmosphere. The northern shore of the lake is a favorite vacation spot for well-to-do Mexicans and Americans while the southern shore is composed of small towns and villages. Lake Chapala is known for its beautiful sunsets and temperate weather. The lake is bordered by mountains, which maintain the peace and privacy of the residents.

Dining in Lake Chapala and Ajijic

Lake Chapala and the surrounding areas feature several hundred restaurants that include everything from native Mexican cuisine to Chinese-American cuisine, even Domino's Pizza. From the upscale restaurants to the corner coffee cafes, Lake Chapala offers almost as much selection as you can find here in the United States, and for far less per meal.

Real Estate in Lake Chapala and Ajijic

The real estate market in Lake Chapala is the most organized market in all Mexico. Hundreds of homes are listed for sale, and there is a Multiple Listing Service (MLS) directory; the same type real estate agents use here when searching for home listings. The average property tax is less than $100 a year, and nice homes in good neighborhoods can be purchased between $60,000 and $100,000 or more.

Shopping in Lake Chapala and Ajijic

Lake Chapala is full of small craft shops and handmade gifts. Common items include Cuban and Mexican cigars, jewelry, wrought-iron furniture, blown glass, pottery, and clothing.

Cost of Living in Lake Chapala and Ajijic

One of the largest reasons to consider living in Lake Chapala, besides the beautiful weather and good healthcare, is the cost of living. Approximately 50,000 Americans are living in Guadalajara, and more are now starting to move to Lake Chapala. You can rent a nice house, complete with a maid and a gardener, for as little as $600 a month or less. Lake Chapala is touted as a place where you can live comfortably on Social Security income — not live extravagantly — but comfortably just the same.

Healthcare in Lake Chapala and Ajijic

Three local hospitals are in Lake Chapala. They feature a bilingual staff, 24-hour emergency and ambulance response centers, and complete diagnostic centers. Public and private hospitals are in Guadalajara about 30 minutes away, and some of them are considered world-class. There is also an international airport in Guadalajara, so if you need to fly home in an emergency, you would be about 30 minutes from boarding a plane.

Prescription drugs are less costly in Mexico; all prescriptions, except for controlled substances, are sold over-the-counter.

Private hospitals require private insurance. You can purchase government-sponsored insurance plans for public hospitals as well as private insurance in Lake Chapala. Government insurance costs roughly $350 per couple per year, and private insurance runs upward of $475 per year. Several nursing homes and assisted care facilities are available, which cost less than they do in the United States should you need them.

The Climate of Lake Chapala and Ajijic

The average climate in Lake Chapala ranges from 50 to 80 degrees Fahrenheit, depending on the season.

The Crime Rate of Lake Chapala

The crime rate in Lake Chapala is low, although actual statistics are unavailable. Residents believe it is safer there than in cities in the United States because local crime is often limited to graffiti and petty theft. Tourists tend to be targeted for theft more often than residents, but the overall rate of occurrence is low.

For More Information on Lake Chapala

There is an excellent book called *Mexico's Lake Chapala and Ajijic: The Insider's Guide to the Northshore for International Travelers*. Check it out online at **www.chapalaguide.com** before you buy it. The following Web sites will provide you with more information about the area.

- www.MexicoAdventure.com

- www.MexConnect.com

- www.Retire-to-LakeChapala-Mexico.com

Mazatlan

Mazatlán is the second largest coastal city in Mexico. It hosts one of Mexico's largest ports, where an average of 40 tons of shrimp are processed each year. North of the enormous port are several miles of undisturbed beaches, which bump up to a bustling resort and tourist haven. A large number of the city's 600,000 residents are retirees age 60 and older.

Food and Dining in Mazatlan

Not surprisingly, seafood is the order of the day in Mazatlán. They have some of the freshest shrimp and seafood around at reasonable prices. For those who prefer chicken or beef, there is plenty of that to go around as well. One semi-famous local restaurant even specializes in fondue. Traditional Mexican food prevails, but American culture has had some influence here: steaks, barbeque, spare ribs, and cappuccinos are all available options.

Real Estate in Mazatlan

Beach-front property in Mazatlán currently runs from $100,000 up to $400,000, depending on the location and the proximity to the water. Further inland, housing properties drop to between $50,000 and $100,000.

Shopping in Mazatlán

Shopping in Mazatlán is an adventure into the old world. Street vendors ply their trades, and haggling is expected. Most shopping is not done through the street vendors; they mainly sell to tourists. Mazatlán features several supermarkets and a couple of shopping malls — so do not worry. You will not be forced to haggle over the price of a live chicken unless you want to. There is a large and beautiful shopping center full of mini-boutiques called the La Gran Plaza that features a full food court and sits next door to a Sam's Club.

Additional features of Mazatlán include two world-class golf resorts, a 150-year-old restored opera house, an aquarium, and even bullfights.

The Cost of Living in Mazatlán

If you choose to purchase locally manufactured goods rather than imported goods from the United States, it is possible to live well in Mazatlán on approximately $1000 to $2000 a month. If you wish to buy imported goods and electronics — be warned — they could cost as much as double there as they do here.

Healthcare Options in Mazatlán

The main hospital in Mazatlán is the Clinica Balboa. It is a modern, well-equipped hospital, and ex-American residents who have been treated there claim they received better treatment there than they ever had in the United States because the doctors speak English and make house calls. If word-of-mouth is any indication, they treat patients more like people than the doctors here in the States. Mazatlán is also fast becoming renowned as a place to have expert plastic surgery, and costs far less than in the United States. Just like the rest of Mexico, prescription drugs are readily available over-the-counter, and cost a fraction of what they do in the United States.

The Climate of Mazatlan

Mazatlán enters a heavy rainy season between July and September. The coolest months of the year are January through March, where the temperature averages between 60 and 70 degrees Fahrenheit. The average high temperature June through October is around 85 degrees Fahrenheit.

The Crime Rate in Mazatlan

Mazatlán has an average crime rate for a city of its size. It is considered to be as safe as most cities in the United States. Crime often involves petty theft rather than murder, so in a sense, it is safer than a lot of U.S. cities. Be aware, however, that while cities like Mazatlán and Lake Chapala are considered safe, parts of Mexico as a whole are not. Do your research carefully before you plan a trip to any foreign country, and practice the same normal caution and safety that you would in any new city — especially at night.

The Realities of Mazatlan

Though largely undiscovered by the Western world, Mazatlán is beginning to attract more attention as a potential retirement spot. This will undoubtedly raise prices in the long run as it has in other tourist-prone areas of Mexico. But it is considered one of the most beautiful cities in Mexico, with interesting history, and plenty of activities for tourists and retirees alike.

Visit the following Web sites for more information on retiring in Mazatlán.

- **www.Mazatlan.com.mx**

- **www.AllAboutMazatlan.com**

- **www.MexConnect.com**

- **www.MexicoBuyersGuide.com**

Panama

Panama is known for its cheap real estate, low cost of living, and a government that actively tries to attract retiring Americans by giving them tax breaks and other incentives. American influence in Panama is evident in everything from the shopping malls to the restaurants. It offers all the comforts and security we are used to enjoying here in America.

Panama is a melting pot with an ethnically diverse population and local culture as well. The trip from the United States to Panama takes about four to five hours by plane, and international flights to Miami, Los Angeles, New York, and other cities are available. Panama City even contains ATMs that work with U.S. banks. Traditionally, the crime rate is low, the weather is beautiful, and the people are friendly.

Panama's Currency

Panama's main unit of currency is the US. dollar. Panama has a stable economy that has been tied to the United States' economy since 1903. They do have a common local currency called the balboa, and most places accept the U.S. dollar and the balboa. Panama currently has the lowest inflation rate of any country in Central America. As of this writing, one Panama balboa is equal to one U.S. dollar.

Dining in Panama

Panama is a cultural crossroads. As such, a variety of different cuisines are common, but the most popular are Latin, Chinese, and American. Common American fast food chains sell food there as well; Pizza Hut, KFC, Subway, McDonald's, and Burger King are just a few of the American companies that have opened stores in Panama.

As an interesting side note, the cattle in Panama are still grazed rather than penned and grain-fed like we do in the United States. People believe this results in better-quality beef with more health benefits — although this is not a proven fact.

Real Estate in Panama

Real estate in Panama is becoming more expensive because the secret is out. But beach-front property is still available under $150,000. Panama offers a variety of real estate options. You can purchase a home in thriving Panama City, along its miles of beaches, or deep in the mountains — whatever suits your taste.

Shopping in Panama

Shopping in Panama is comparable to shopping in the United States. There are malls, supermarkets, superstores, and corner convenience stores, just like in the United States, except things often cost less. Panama has three major shopping malls, electronics stores, and just about anything else you can think of. They claim their high-speed Internet service is better than we have here in the United States. At the very least, Internet service is available and inexpensive.

Cost of Living in Panama

Retired residents of Panama suggest that you can live comfortably for around $2000 to $3000 a month. By "comfortably," they mean a close equivalent to the average American lifestyle. Here are more specific examples of what things cost in Panama.

- Outside a major city, you can rent an apartment for as little as $150 a month. Inside the cities, this number rises to between $300 and $500 a month.

- Housekeepers can be hired for around $10 a day and to $120 a month if they are live-in.

- A pound of frozen vegetables costs just under $1, and a loaf of bread is about 69 cents.

- Three pounds of laundry detergent costs an average of $3.

- One pound of beef is around $2, while a pound of chicken is about $1.

Healthcare in Panama

Panama features several U.S.-quality hospitals, and most everyone speaks English. Doctors in Panama are often trained in the United States. Healthcare is often comparable to the quality of care found here. Private health insurance is available and is far cheaper than the premiums we often pay here.

Climate in Panama

Panama experiences a May to November rainy season where the average is an inch of rain a day. The average temperature in Panama City is between 76 and 86 degrees Fahrenheit, but it is often warmer. Locations further into the mountains tend to have more spring-like weather year-round.

Crime in Panama

Crime is low in Panama. Compared to other countries in the region Panama, as a whole, has the highest rating for tourist safety and the lowest crime rate in general.

Special Benefits for Retirees in Panama

The Panamanian government encourages retirees to move to Panama with the now famous Pencionado Program.

Benefits include:

- A 50 percent discount on closing costs for home loans
- 25 percent off at restaurants
- 25 percent off airline tickets
- 10 percent off prescription medications
- 15 percent off dental and eye exams
- 30 to 50 percent off hotel rooms.

These are just a few benefits of the Pencionado Program. To qualify for these discounts, all you have to do is show your retiree visa. The visa is obtained when you provide proof of a monthly income (at least $500), a police report, and a health certificate.

The Realities of Panama

While the beautiful climate, the easily accepted dollar, and lower real estate prices make Panama look attractive, you should be aware of a few things before you consider moving there.

It is more difficult to open a bank account in Panama than it is in the United States. In the U.S., there is competition for our money. We are used to fee-free checking accounts, no minimum balances, and even being able to open our accounts online. In Panama, you have to cut through red tape before you can open an account. You will have to bring in your passport, a letter from your bank in the United States, references from people you know in Panama, your credit history, and other things. There are also minimum balance requirements for even normal checking accounts.

One other thing to remember is that Panama is still a developing country. Because of their close interaction with the United States, they have amenities that other developing countries do not, but they are still subject to power outages, water shortages, and things of that nature.

For more information on Panama, visit these Web sites:

- **www.YourPanama.com**
- **www.RetireInPanama.info**

Ecuador

Ecuador's different climates range from the sunny beaches of the Galapagos Islands to snowy, silent, and imposing volcanoes, and even the jungles of the Amazon. Ecuador is a small country (about the size of Colorado), but it has long been considered one of the best places in the world to retire. It has gained even more popularity in recent years. Combine the low cost of real estate with truly beautiful climates, and you have what just might be called "a magical retiree paradise."

Ecuador's Currency

The U.S. dollar is the local currency of Ecuador, though they do produce their own coins.

Dining in Ecuador

The two main cities, Quito and Guayaquil, offer a variety of restaurant options. Seafood is cheap and popular, and gourmet and ethnic restaurants are available to the discerning traveler. Outside of the main cities, ethnic food prevails.

Ecuadorian tastes, however, do not always mesh with what we are used to eating here in the United States. Some of the local dishes are appealing: ceviche de camarones is a local specialty of shrimp cooked in lemon juice served with onions and parsley. Other common dishes include tropical fruits, potato pancakes called tortilla de papas, and a sugar cane drink called aguardiente. Less appetizing local dishes include roasted cuy (guinea pig) and tronquito (bull penis soup).

Real Estate in Ecuador

Ecuador offers beachfront property for as low as $38,000. Prices are often higher, but if you take the time to look, you can find some real bargains in real estate. At the time of this writing, you could purchase an entire mountain (38,000 square feet) in Ecuador for about $400,000. Ecuador does offer one of the most beautiful and reasonable places in the world to begin your retirement. Plots of beachfront property without a pre-built home on them are selling for as little as $10,000.

Shopping in Ecuador

The capital city of Quito features six shopping malls, as well as artisan fairs and street vendors. It is a city beginning to modernize, but it has not yet been hit with the massive corporate conglomerations that we take for granted here in America. There are several supermarkets in Quito with almost everything a tourist would want or need to buy. One of the best features of the local economy is the fresh vegetables and meats sold at the local markets. Ecuadorians are not as removed from their food as we are, and you can find food that is less tampered with and fresher than in our supermarkets here.

The Cost of Living in Ecuador

The cost of housing and rental properties in the main cities can range between $500 and $1000 per month. If you are willing to move out of the main cities, the cost lowers dramatically, down to around $250 per month and up. Quito is considered one of the least costly cities in the world to live in.

Healthcare in Ecuador

The larger cities in Ecuador offer hospitals, ambulance services, clinics, and maternity services. The farther you get from the main cities, the more remote the hospitals are. If you choose to consider living in Ecuador, you may wish to purchase emergency evacuation insurance, which could help you get back to the United States quickly if you needed treatment.

The Climate in Ecuador

Ecuador boasts different climates within its four main regions. The coastal lowlands of the west are warm, with a rainy season that lasts from December to May. The La Sierra Highlands are mountainous and cooler. The temperature there varies with the altitude. The Amazon region in east Ecuador is what you would expect from a rainforest — humid and rainy. The Amazon region's dry season is between November and February. The Galapagos Islands are warm, dry, and beautiful almost year-round.

The Crime Rate in Ecuador

An estimated half of the cocaine bound for the United States passes from Colombia through the waters around Ecuador. It is something the Ecuadorian government tries to prohibit, but it still happens. That being said, the overall crime rate within Ecuador is reported to be lower than in most industrialized countries.

Visit these Web sites for more information about retiring in Ecuador.

- **www.ExpatExchange.com**
- **www.TheBestofEcuador.com**

Belize

Belize is located on the east coast of Central America. It is bordered by Guatemala to the south, Mexico to the north, and the Caribbean Sea to the east. It includes 266 square miles of islands and the longest barrier reef in the Western Hemisphere — over 180 miles long. It has a truly spectacular climate with an average yearly temperature of 79 degrees Fahrenheit. Main attractions include the ancient Mayan cities within its borders. English is the primary language of Belize, but Spanish and Creole are also spoken.

The Currency of Belize

The Belize dollar is the most common unit of currency, and has a fixed rate of exchange with the U.S. dollar. One U.S. dollar equals two Belize dollars. Hotels and tourist establishments accept the U.S. dollar as well as the Belize dollar.

Dining in Belize

The staple foods for many in Belize are red beans and rice, stewed fish, lobster, and an onion broth soup called "escabeche." Fresh coconut and coconut milk are popular food additives, and vendors sell tamales, fried fish cakes, and more.

Eating out in Belize can involve everything from a trip to a local club to one of the small restaurants that line the streets. Seafood is a huge staple on the menu, but restaurants serve beef and chicken as well. You can find American-style food there, too: muffins, lattes, pizza, and fried chicken are readily available. Fine wines and cheese are available at specialty stores there just as they are here.

Real Estate in Belize

Untouched lots in Belize can run between $25,000 and $50,000, while the average home off the beach costs between $35,000 and $100,000, depending on the size of the home and the neighborhood. Homes within Belize City run the gamut between $35,000 and $350,000. Rentals for secure, two story American-style houses run from $300 a month upwards.

Shopping in Belize

Gas is slightly more expensive in Belize, but it is one of the only things that is higher. Most food comes from local farmers. Vendors come regularly to set up stalls at the local markets, and fresh fruits, vegetables, and meats are available year-round. Belize City contains modern supermarkets, however, these are often absent or few and far between.

The Cost of Living in Belize

An income of $1000 to $2000 a month can buy a nice life in Belize in some of the best, most exciting areas it has to offer, including waterfront areas. Prices in the developing retirement communities may cost slightly more, but offer more of the American amenities that we are used to having.

Healthcare in Belize

Private health insurance is limited in Belize, but it is growing. Most private health insurance companies are extensions of larger international companies. There also is a developing government-sponsored healthcare system. Within the main cities healthcare is readily available, though it will not be the same experience you might expect here in the United States. If you choose to travel or live in Belize, you will want to purchase evacuation insurance to help you get back to the United States in the event of an emergency. Expatriates living in Belize often fly to Houston or Miami for care.

The Climate in Belize

Belize experiences a rainy season from June to November each year, and a dry temperate season between February and May. The average annual temperature is approximately 79 degrees Fahrenheit.

The Crime Rate in Belize

Crime in Belize is common in the poorer parts of Belize City and some of its smaller outlying villages. If you are considering retiring to Belize, vacation and rent there frequently so that you will have enough knowledge about the undesirable neighborhoods before you buy a house in one by mistake.

Special Retirement Benefits in Belize

Like Panama Belize offers special incentives to retiring expatriates. Though the program is not as well developed and does not offer as many incentives, the ones it does offer are huge.

Anyone 45 years or older can qualify for their special retirement program. There are some restrictions: People wishing to qualify for Belize's retirement program must submit proof of a $2000 a month pension or annuity that is generated outside of Belize and submit to a background check.

The retirement program has two main benefits. When you first arrive in Belize, you are qualified to import all your personal articles, even your car, tax- and duty-free. Any income or investment earnings you make from a source outside Belize are tax-free.

Two retirement communities are located within Belize. They are located in the Corozal District and the Punta Gorda District. The Punta Gorda District offers a gated community next to beautiful Mayan ruins, where you can enjoy local waterfalls, caverns, and the ruins themselves, as well as sports like kayaking, fishing, and hiking. The river is deep, and special accommodations have been made so that you can pull a boat right up to your home. All the homes within the village are built according to United States' standards.

More information on Belize can be found on the Internet at **www. BelizeRetirement.org.**

The Republic of Malta

The Republic of Malta is comprised of five islands in the Mediterranean Sea just south of Italy. It is a cherished retirement spot for many of Europe's seniors.

Malta's landscape is truly the "stuff dreams are made of." The shorelines of the five islands boast secluded lagoons and miles of pristine beaches. English and Maltese are the national languages, with 98 percent of the population speaking English.

The Currency of Malta

On January 1, 2008, Malta adopted the Euro as its official unit of currency. As of this writing one Euro is currently equal to 1.6 U.S. dollars.

Dining in Malta

The Republic of Malta features a rich and glorious history. Many countries have claimed the Maltese islands as their own at one point or another. Their Arab, Roman, French, and British conquerors left their mark not only on the buildings on the islands, but in their cuisines as well.

American fast food style restaurants are plentiful, but the true joy comes in experiencing Malta's native fare. Among the traditional options you will find Italian dishes most prevalent. Dishes such as fish soup, bean dip, ratatouille, beef olives, date slices, cream filled cannoli, and even macaroni, are all standard Maltese fare.

Real Estate in Malta

Housing in Malta can be expensive depending on the style of house you choose, and the location. Although houses cannot be had for bargain basement prices, there is still one big benefit to buying a home there — you do not have to pay property taxes.

If you intend to purchase property in Malta, you will have to apply for a government permit. Strict building codes are enforced to protect both the culture and quality of life in the islands.

Shopping in Malta

Open air markets are the standard in Malta, with vendors selling everything from fresh vegetables to snacks of dates, olives and even bottles of wine. There are plenty of clothing stores which feature the latest European fashions, and small cafes where you can sit and relax. You will see few large department stores or supermarkets. Instead you can expect small boutiques, bakeries and handmade goods.

The Cost of Living in Malta

The cost of living in Malta is slightly higher than in many popular retirement countries because there is currently an 18 percent tax on all imported products. The average cost of a gallon of milk is $1.30, and housing costs vary. Homes usually cost upwards of $100,000.

Healthcare in Malta

Malta includes both a public and a private healthcare system. Public hospitals are funded by the government, and residents can receive care for free. Prescriptions, however, are not free. Private hospitals work much like those in the United States and visits must be paid by private health insurance.

Healthcare in Malta is excellent and readily available. The Maltese government and the individual hospitals are working together to improve the standards of care each year. Should you decide that you need to receive medical care outside Malta, many of the major European cities are between 2 and 4 hours away by plane.

Climate in Malta

The average temperature in Malta is 64 degrees. April through August is sunny and dry. Their rainy season falls between October and March. Their winters are mild, and they rarely get snow.

Crime in Malta

Statistically, Malta has a lower crime rate than many parts of the United States. It is considered a very safe place to live.

Visit **www.RetireMalta.com** for more information.

Costa Rica

The Currency of Costa Rica

Some places in Costa Rica do accept the U.S. dollar, but the primary unit of currency is the colón or colones — plural.

At the time of this writing one U.S. dollar was worth roughly 503 colones.

Dining in Costa Rica

Costa Rican cuisine relies heavily on rice and beans. Costa Rican cattle are grass-fed and beef, chicken, and fish are the main meat options. Vegetables are not always included with native meals, but are readily available. American-style restaurants are nearly as common as the native establishments within the major cities.

Popular Costa Rican Dishes include:

- Papas con Chorizo - Chorizo sausage with potatoes

- Barbudos - String bean omelet

- Frito - Pork Stew

- Arroz Guacho - Sticky rice

- Higado en salsa - Beef liver salsa

- Mondongo - Beef Stomach Soup.

Real Estate in Costa Rica

The average cost of a home in Costa Rica ranges between $40,000 and $80,000 depending on the size of the home and the location.

Shopping in Costa Rica

Bartering is a way of life in Costa Rica, and if you are skilled, many everyday items can be had at a serious discount. Imported items, especially electronics, are a different story. Stereos, computers, etc., can often cost far more in Costa Rica than they do in the United States. The best policy is to bring any electronic items with you when you move, rather than trying to purchase them once you are in the country.

The Cost of Living in Costa Rica

Costa Rica is the most expensive place to live in all of Latin America. That said, it is still a bargain compared to the cost of living in the United States. A couple can expect to live very well on as little as $1200 a month in Costa Rica. If you can afford upwards of $2000 a month, then you can have a life of considerable luxury. Many people in Costa Rica live on far less than $1200 a month and still have an excellent quality of life since housing and utilities there cost far less than they do here.

Healthcare in Costa Rica

Healthcare in Costa Rica is very close to the same standard of care we expect here in the United States. Government sponsored insurance is available to everyone, not just natives, for a monthly fee that is based on your income. A network of 29 hospitals and over 250 clinics, known as the Caja Costarricense de Seguro Social (CCSS), are responsible for the majority of care Costa

Rican citizens receive. If you do not wish to use public hospitals or clinics, private care is also available. Private care is more expensive, but it is easy to get.

Climate in Costa Rica

Costa Rica has a beautiful tropical climate. The average annual temperatures range from 71 to 81 degrees. The wettest months are July and November. They are occasionally subject to severe storms but for the most part, the weather is beautiful.

Crime in Costa Rica

Crime is on the rise in Costa Rica, with gangs being the number one concern of many citizens, particularly in San Jose. Costa Rica is still considered a very safe place to live though, and the government is constantly finding new ways to help lower the crime rates. Even with the rising concern over violent crimes, Costa Rica is still statistically considered a safer place to live than many areas in the United States.

For more information on Costa Rica visit: **http://www.retireincostarica.net/**

Emergency Evacuation Insurance

Emergency medical evacuation insurance is a form of travel insurance that you purchase in case you need to return to the United States quickly. If you plan to travel or retire to a foreign country, it is an important investment to consider.

This type of insurance is concerned with paying for the cost of getting you back to the hospital of your choice as quickly as possible. If the worst were to happen and you or a loved one needed to charter a private flight or travel by helicopter to get to the hospital, you would be covered. Even if you were able to take a regular flight back to the States, you could be forced to purchase extra seats to hold medical equipment or attendants. The cost of the immediate, unplanned travel expense could end up being well over a hundred thousand dollars. Or worse, you could be forced to accept medical care in a foreign country, simply because you could not afford to get back home.

Emergency evacuation insurance is not cheap, but it can give you peace of mind if you are living outside the United States. Different types of policies are available, including group policies. If you are friends with other expatriates in your new country, that may be something you can go in on together.

If you would like more information on emergency evacuation policies, visit **www.TravelInsure.com**. This site provides a list of emergency evacuation policies, and you can compare prices to find the right one for you and your family.

Retire for Less in the United States

Even if you are not ready to take the plunge and retire overseas, plenty of places right here in America welcome retirees, have amazing healthcare, and offer a slightly lower cost of living.

1) Walla Walla, Washington

CNN Money ranked Walla Walla, Washington, the number one place to retire in America due to its low population (approx 30,000 people) and reasonable real estate. Walla Walla also has a growing and increasingly active retired community focused on good times. Some are even pursuing higher education at the local colleges.

The median home price in Walla Walla is $175,000, and the city scored well for safety; the crime rate is 26 points lower than the national average. The climate in Walla Walla varies from an average low of 28 degrees Fahrenheit in January to an average high of 89 degrees Fahrenheit in July.

Residents of Walla Walla are proud of their burgeoning wine industry, and the city is quickly becoming known as a peaceful place to relax, sit back, and enjoy the best that life has to offer.

2) St. Simons Island, Georgia

This tiny island is about five miles off the coast of Brunswick, Georgia. The word is out about St. Simons Island, and it has a large number of retirees within its small population of 13,000. Sandy beaches and restaurants abound as well as some limited marshland for the adventurous. Because of the recent attention St. Simons has received home prices are on the rise; homes currently sell for about $300,000 and up. The weather ranges from an average low of 49 degrees Fahrenheit in January to an average high of 90 degrees Fahrenheit in July. The average age of its residents is 46.

3) Virginia Beach, Virginia

Virginia Beach is a growing city with a population of more than 430,000 people. It features 38 miles of waterfront, fine dining, entertainment, and reasonable available housing. The average home price is around $200,000.

4) Prescott, Arizona

Active retirees will love Prescott, Arizona. The small town has seven golf courses and features more than 450 miles of hiking trails within the Prescott National Forest. With a population of about 40,000 people, the city is big enough to have all the amenities you are used to and small enough for you to comfortably get to know the people around you. The average home price is around $250,000, and there are some state tax incentives for retirees.

5) Portsmouth, New Hampshire

Portsmouth features bustling markets, fresh lobster dinners, theaters, and even a music hall. It was rated one of the ten safest places in America by *Places Rated Almanac*, and the city offers the charm of a close community and the privacy of a larger growing city. Housing prices have risen recently due to a swell of newcomers, but the current average price of housing there is around $200,000.

Moving during retirement may not sound like the most appealing option at first, but there are clear benefits to making your dollar stretch further during your retirement years. Even if you plan to spend your days right where you are, you can always lower your cost of living. Consider carefully the implications of moving overseas before you do it — especially where medical care is concerned. If you choose to live or travel overseas, please make sure that you purchase emergency evacuation insurance.

If you are looking for more information on where the best places to retire are, visit **www.WhereToRetire.com**. It is the official Web site of *Where to Retire* magazine, a monthly publication that features prime retirement areas inside and outside the U.S.

Where to Retire takes a close look at conditions that concern retirees and features in-depth articles about some of the most beautiful places in the world at home and abroad. You can visit them on the Internet and request a free issue of the magazine. Also available are free brochures and information from the magazine's sponsors. If you are considering moving during retirement, *Where to Retire* magazine offers you a way to consider all your options and presents it in a fun, easy-to-read format.

Case Study: Where to Retire

With a circulation of over 500,000 readers Where to Retire Magazine is fast becoming the foremost authority on retirement relocation.

Where to Retire Magazine is filled with vital information for those looking to relocate when they retire. The magazine covers issues like local climates, state and local taxes, housing costs, health care and many other things you need to know before you decide where to spend your retirement years.

Books, special reports, and back issues of Where to Retire Magazine are available for sale through the **WhereToRetire.com** Web site.

When you visit the Web site you can request a free issue of the magazine, as well as plenty of free brochures and information on locations like Panama, Costa Rica, and Mexico.

You can check them out on the web at **www.WhereToRetire.com**

14

Putting It All Together: Your Unique Retirement Solution

Projected Retirement Income Worksheet

After all the discussion about ways to cut spending, pay off debt, and begin investing, it is time to turn the attention to you. This chapter will focus on your plan for retirement, your investments, and how long they are going to last.

You need to know that these will be projections at best. The further away from retirement you are, the more difficult it will be to predict how much money you will have. Things like inflation, and how well your investments will compound cannot be predicted perfectly. This worksheet purposely does not figure in taxes. Once you have completed it, you should have a good idea of which tax bracket you will fall into and be able to figure it out from there.

Now, to be fair, this worksheet makes two big assumptions.

- That your investments will not lose value

- That your investments will not gain value

I strongly suggest that you use a compound interest calculator as you work through the following pages. Not doing so could seriously undervalue the amount of money available to you at retirement. To find a compound interest calculator online, search Google for the words "compound interest calculator" and check the links until you find one you like.

You can still get an accurate picture of where you want to go, and how soon you are going to be able to get there if you take the time to work through this section carefully; especially if you use a compound interest calculator as you go.

This is simple math. It is addition, subtraction, multiplication and division, with a few percentages thrown in. Do not talk yourself out of doing these formulas. You can do it, and it is the best way to learn what your estimated monthly income will be in retirement.

The best thing you can do is make copies of these pages and put them in your financial journal. Review them once a year when you rebalance your portfolio. This way, you can see that you are still on track and progressing toward your goals. Many answers here may require some research on your part. That is all right. Do the sections you can now, and then take a break. This is not a test like the Scholastic Assessment Test (SAT); it is a way for you to sit down and consciously take into account all your possible income sources during retirement and figure out how long each of them will last you.

Taking the time to sit down and work through these sections now will save you years of worry and speculation about whether or not you will be able to retire. It will also answer the big questions, "What will my monthly income be?" and "When should I start accessing this account or that one?"

Let us start with the big question: How old will you be when you retire? If you do not know the exact date, list the age you would like to retire.

Estimated retirement age: _____

Now subtract your retirement age from 100 to get the number of years your money needs to last you. We may not all live to be 100, but no one plans to go sooner, so why not plan on those extra years so that you can be sure your money will last as long as you do? For example, if you plan to retire at 68, your formula would look like this: 100 − 68 = 32. Your investments are going to need to last at least 32 years.

Setting your needed number of years above the average life expectancy gives you a cushion of money. After all, what if something beyond your control happened to you in your retirement years? What if your house was hit with a terrible storm or you had a costly medical emergency? It is better to be withdraw less than you need to regularly, so money will be in reserve for emergencies. Adjust this number according to your own needs.

The number of years that my retirement money is going to have to last me is: _____

Employer Sponsored Pensions

If you are lucky enough to get a pension from your current employer, how old will you need to be to start collecting it? If you are unsure, check with your human resources department. Ask them what the average monthly pension amount from your company is, and list it here. If you are to get a lump-sum pension, it is assumed you will be rolling it over into another type of account.

If you plan to keep a lump-sum pension someplace that is accessible, like a savings account, write the total lump sum you will receive here:

Lump sum pension payment amount: _____

Next, divide this lump sum by the number of years that your retirement money needs to last.

Example: $50,000 divided by 32 years = $1562.50 per year (rounded). Now, divide that number by 12, for the 12 months in each year for a monthly total. $1562/12 = $130.20 per month.

That number will be the amount of money you can safely withdraw from your lump-sum pension each month without running out of money. For some of you, your company will do this automatically and you will have no say over it. In that case, just enter the amount you will receive monthly.

Monthly allotted withdrawals from my pension plan:

_____

Now, this is not much money monthly, but we are going to factor in your income from other places as well. This is simply the amount of money you can safely withdraw each month without stealing from your future retirement needs. This is done also just to give you a general idea, because it does not factor in any amount of interest you may earn over the years; interest earned by keeping that money in a savings account or other investment venue.

We are going to do the same thing for each of your investment accounts. At the end, we will add them together to see what your estimated monthly income will look like in retirement.

401(k), 403(b), and Comparable Accounts

If you are participating in a 401(k) plan, a 403(b) plan, or a comparable retirement savings plan at work, let us work through it here.

The amount you are going to have available to you when you retire will depend on the contributions you make while you are still working.

As of 2008, you are allowed to contribute up to $15,500 to your 401(k) accounts yearly ($20,550 if you are over 50 years old). Again, this formula ignores the effects of any interest your investments may earn and uses only the estimated total amount of money you will contribute to this plan between now and then. For a more accurate total, use a compound interest calculator.

The current amount in your 401(k) account: _____

How much do you plan to contribute each year until you retire? _____

How many years away is your desired retirement age? _____

_____

Multiply the amount you plan to contribute each year by the number of years you have left before retirement.

Example: I have 15 years left until I retire and I plan to contribute $10,000 a year to my 401(k). $10,000 × 15 years = $150,000 that I will contribute between now and retirement.

Add that to what is already in your retirement account to get an estimate of the amount you will be retiring on. $150,000 + $2,200 that I have already paid into my 401(k) plan = $152,200.

This is why you need to use a compound interest calculator. If I contribute $10,000 a year to my 401(k) account for the next 15 years, and those investments earn even 5 percent, at retirement, I will have $231,148.56 in my 401(k) account, not $150,000.

Now take the estimated amount you will have at retirement and divide it by the number of years you need it to last. You cannot access your 401(k) account without penalty until you reach 59 and a half.

Example: My $152,200 needs to last me 32 years: $152,200 divided by 32 = $4756 a year. Each year has 12 months, so $4756 divided by 12 = $396 dollar per month.

Variables

The IRS will undoubtedly raise the contribution limit in the future. For now, just use the numbers that you have. If something changes, come back to this section and re-do your calculations.

If your employer matches a percentage of your contributions each year, do not forget to factor this in.

Example: I am going to contribute $10,000 a year to my 401(k) plan. My employer matches 5 percent of my contributions each year up to $1000 $10,000 x 5% (0.05) = $500 so my yearly contribution amount will be $10,500 a year.

Do not forget that once you are over 50, you are allowed to make an additional "catch up" contribution of up to $5,000. If you are putting the maximum allowable into your 401(k), be sure you include the additional $5,000 for each year that you contribute once you are over 50.

Write the total amount that you can safely withdraw each month from your 401(k) account here: _____

Annuities

If you purchased or are in the process of purchasing an annuity, read your contract to find out how much you will receive each month and for how long.

Date that my annuity payments will start: _____

Date that my annuity payments will end: _____

Monthly amount of the annuity: _____

IRA Accounts

As of 2008, you can contribute up to $5,000 per year if you are under 50 years old, and up to $6,000 per year if you are over 50.

Amount currently in your IRA accounts: _____

The amount you are going to contribute to your IRA accounts yearly: _____

Number of years you will have to contribute until retirement: _____

Total amount that will be available in your IRA accounts at retirement: _____

If necessary, use a compound interest calculator to figure out the total available amount.

Example: I currently have $10,000 in my IRA account. I have 15 years until retirement. I plan to contribute the maximum allowable amount each year until I retire at 68. Since I am over 50, I can contribute $6,000 per year for the next 15 years. I hope that my investments will earn at least a 5 percent return over the next 15 years.

The Basic Math

15 years × $6,000 per year = $90,000. Add the $10,000 that I currently have in my IRA, and I will have $100,000 at retirement. Using a compound interest calculator to figure in the 5 percent

gain each year means that I will have $156,734 at retirement.

Next, divide the total that will be available by the number of years you will spend in retirement. In my example, I will need my money to last 32 years.

$156,734 divided by 32 years = $4897 per year.

$4897 divided by 12 months = $408 a month.

The wonderful thing about interest is that it will continue to grow, even when you start making withdrawals. Continuing to let your investments compound during retirement is the most essential thing you can do. Do not remove things in a lump sum and put them in your checking account. Take these periodic payments, and allow the rest to continue to grow within secure investments like CDs, bonds, and so on. Better yet, continue to let them grow tax-deferred in an IRA or 401(k) account.

You must begin taking withdrawals from a traditional IRA account at age 70 and a half. Roth IRA accounts have no date that you are required to begin withdrawing from them.

Personal Investment Accounts

If you have personal investment accounts that you plan to use during retirement, factor them into the equation here.

For example, I contribute $50 a month to an individual stock account through ShareBuilder.com. I have this money unofficially earmarked for retirement. Assuming that I continue to contribute $50 a month ($600 a year) for the next 15 years, I will have $9,000 in that account for retirement. If my investments earn 5 percent interest, I will have $13,594 in the account at retirement. It is not much, but it will help supplement an emergency or give me additional monthly income when I need it.

Total amount of money available from personal accounts at retirement: _____

If you have enough that you wish to add it to your monthly income, factor it here: _____

Total monthly income from personal accounts: _____

Social Security

Social Security will be a little different. The Social Security Administration will figure out how much money you get monthly based on your contributions while you worked. To figure out what your estimated Social Security payments will be in retirement, visit their Web site and use their online calculator. Their Web site is located at **www.SSA.gov.**

Do not forget that if you participate in Medicare, your premiums will be deducted from your Social Security check. This will lower your monthly income.

Estimated monthly Social Security payment: _____

Bonds, CDs, and Securities

It may be difficult to factor a monthly income total for money that you have in these types of securities. Since they will all have different maturity dates, the money will not be available to you until the investment matures. However, you may find it helpful to go ahead and figure out how much you could withdraw from these investments monthly if you needed to. This will help you stagger the maturity dates as you near retirement.

Example: If I have $40,000 between CDs and T-bills, and I need the money to last 32 years, I can withdraw $1250 a year from these types of accounts. That would likely mean cashing out one $1000 CD a year (plus any interest it earned).

A one-year $1000 CD that earned 5 percent interest would be worth $1050 when I cashed it out. Dividing the $1050 by 12 months gives me $87 a month in additional retirement income.

Estimated monthly income from bonds, CDs, and other securities: _____

Supplemental Retirement Income

If you have decided to pursue a working retirement, you will have supplemental income. While it is difficult to know how much you can earn this far in advance, go ahead and estimate what you think you are capable of earning each month.

If you are earning money as an independent contractor, or in any form in which taxes are not already taken out of your check, you must set aside 30 percent of your income in a savings account for taxes. The best bet is to put it into a high-yield savings account. At least you will get to keep the interest it earns there.

Expected monthly income from supplemental sources: _____

After taxes, if necessary: _____

Total Monthly Income During Retirement

We are going to put everything together now and see how much you can reasonably afford to withdraw from each of your investments each month.

Monthly total from a pension: _____

Monthly total from a 401(k) account: _____

Monthly total from annuities: _____

Monthly total from an IRA account: _____

Monthly total from personal accounts: _____

Monthly total from Social Security: _____

Monthly total from bonds and securities: _____

Monthly supplemental income total: _____

Add them all together: _____

Total monthly income during retirement $ _____

This number may be higher or lower than your needs, but at least you have a ballpark figure for how much you are going to have access to each month during your retirement. Congratulate yourself for taking the time to go over these formulas; you are far more prepared now than you were. Hopefully, this has helped you to identify areas where you are progressing better than you thought you were, as well as places and accounts that you need to begin contributing to if you are not already.

If you would like more information on retirement calculators, visit the following Web sites: **www.CNNMoney.com, www. Bloomberg.com, www.MoneyChimp.com.**

"Retire from work, but not from life."

M.K. Soni

Conclusion

I hope this book has helped you begin charting the course for your retirement. There is nothing worse than worrying that your golden years will crumble and fall away because you cannot support yourself financially. If you take nothing else away from this book, please take the following advice.

No matter how close to retirement you are, there is still time to change old habits and save money for your future.

The surest way to wealth is to become a lender rather than a borrower. If you are still carrying high balances on your credit cards and making frequent impulse purchases, stop and give yourself some room to breathe. It will be a terrible, terrible mistake to carry your debt into retirement. If you will honestly evaluate your habits, chances are you can make enough changes to support your retirement without ever feeling deprived.

Do not beat yourself up over a lack of savings. We all wish we could go back and talk to our younger selves and teach them a thing or two, but we cannot. All you can do is deal with where you are right now, today.

Today is one more step on the path to a comfortable, secure retirement. Where you go from here is up to you.

"Age is an issue of mind over matter. If you don't mind, it doesn't matter."

Mark Twain

Bibliography

Armstrong, Elizabeth. *America's Best Places to Retire: Fourth Edition: The Only Guide You Need to Today's Top Retirement Towns (America's 100 Best Places to Retire)*. USA: Vacation Publications, 2007.

Brock, Fred. *Retire on Less Than You Think: The New York Times Guide To Planning Your Future.* USA: Times Books, 2004.

Cilley, Marla. *Sink Reflections: Overwhelmed? Disorganized? Living in Chaos? The FlyLady's Simple FLYing Lessons Will Show You How to Get Your Home and Your Life in Order — and It All Starts with Shining Your Sink!* USA: Bantam, 2002

Cullinane, Jan and Cathy Fitzgerald. *The New Retirement: The Ultimate Guide to the Rest of Your Life.* United States: Rodale Press, 2004.

Ely, Leanne. "How to Put the Food Budget on a Diet" Saving Dinner.**http://www.savingdinner.com/archives/articles/how_to_put_the_food_budget_on_a_diet.html** (15 Dec. 2007).

"Personal Budget Software — Excel Budgeting Template, Free Personal Finance Spreadsheets" You Need A Budget.**http://www.youneedabudget.com/** (27 Nov. 2007).

Ruffenach, Glenn and Kelly Greene. *The Wall Street Journal Complete Retirement Guidebook*. New York: Three Rivers Press, 2007.

Savage, Terry. *The Savage Number: How Much Money Do You Need To Retire?* New Jersey: John Wiley and Sons, Inc., 2005.

Schlossberg, Nancy K. *Retire Smart, Retire Happy: Finding Your True Path in Life*. USA: American Psychological Association (APA), 2003.

Sedlar, Jeri, and Rick Miners. *Don't Retire, Rewire*, 2nd Edition. USA: Alpha, 2007.

Stein, Ben and Paul Demuth. *Yes, You Can Still Retire Comfortably*. USA: New Beginnings Press, 2005.

"Where to Retire Magazine" Where to Retire. **http://www.wheretoretire.com/** (1 Jan. 2008).

Zelinski Ernie L. *How to Retire Happy Wild and Free: Retirement Wisdom That You Won't Get From Your Financial Advisor*. USA: Ten Speed Press, 2004.

Author Biography

Connie Brooks is the owner and operator of Thrifty Mamas.com. It is a Web site dedicated to helping you protect your family and save some of your hard earned money at the same time. She invites you to join her on the Web at **www.ThriftyMamas.com.**

"Don't simply retire from something; have something to retire to."

Harry Emerson Fosdick

Glossary

401(k): A 401(k) plan is an employer-sponsored retirement fund that allows any participants to contribute money from their salary in a tax-deferred fashion.

403(b) plan: A tax sheltered annuity offered to tax-exempt employees (including those who work for the public school system). The employer may defer taxes on his or her contribution.

Actual Deferral Percentage: A test that looks at how much of a paycheck is deferred to a retirement plan for highly compensated employees versus how much is contributed by non highly compensated employees.

Adjusted Gross Income (AGI): Your total income (before taxes) minus any adjustments to your income.

After-Tax: Any contributions made to your retirement account that are deducted from your paycheck after taxes have been taken out.

American Stock Exchange (AMEX): Trades only small- to mid-sized stocks in addition to options and exchange-traded funds.

Annuities: Regular payments from a retirement account or insurance company that holds your annuity contract.

Asset Class: Securities that behave similarly on the market and share similar characteristics. There are generally three types: equities (stocks), fixed-income (bonds) and cash equivalents (money market funds).

Automatic Enrollment: An employer-sponsored plan that automatically opens a retirement savings account for eligible employees. The employee does not need to sign up for this plan and can opt-out from contributing any money by submitting a form to human resources.

Bear Market: A market where stock prices are down significantly.

Beneficiary: The person, persons, or fund that will receive the money in your 401(k) or other retirement account in the event of your death.

Beta: The risk of a single investment compared to the risk of the market as a whole.

Blue-Chip Stocks: A stable investment because the companies considered to be blue-chip are normally older and have established themselves in the market. All stocks listed in the Dow Jones Industrial Average fall into this category.

Brokerage Window: May be offered by your employer, it lets you invest in things outside of what is offered by your company (otherwise known as a self-directed option). This often comes at an extra fee, and you should be very careful if you have one.

Often, people believe they can use the brokerage window for day trading, but not many use it successfully to make quick money (this is also the reason why many employers do not offer this option).

Bull Market: A market where stock prices rise significantly.

Cafeteria Plan: A plan that allows employees to choose from a diverse menu of benefits

Cash or Deferred Arrangement (CODA): A 401(k) plan or similar retirement plan where an employee is able to make contributions to an employer-offered account.

Cash Profit Sharing Plan: A plan with a menu of choices including cash options or other benefits.

Certificate of Deposit: A CD, as it is commonly known, is offered by a bank, but unlike a bank account, you are required to leave your money in the CD for a set amount of time. At the end of that term, you will receive your initial investment plus an interest rate that was guaranteed at the start of the CD's term. Often, this interest rate is higher than that of a savings account.

Compensation: Something you earn from working (including tips and bonuses, for example).

Compounding: Earning interest on your interest (another benefit of a long-term investment).

Defined Benefit Plans: A retirement plan sponsored by your employer. Investments are controlled by your employer, and benefits are divvied out using a formula that includes salary history and how long you have been with your employer. May also be known as qualified benefit plans and non-qualified benefit plans.

Defined Contribution Plans: A retirement plan in which your employer sets aside a certain amount of money each year for your retirement.

Department of Labor: A federal agency that helps to ensure that workers across the country have adequate working conditions, pay, opportunities for employment, benefits, etc. They ensure that collective bargaining can take place and administer laws regarding wages, discrimination, unemployment, and safe working conditions.

Determination Letter: A document from the IRS that states that a retirement plan meets IRS requirements for tax-advantaged treatment.

Direct Transfer: A tax-free transfer of retirement savings funds from one account sponsor to another (for example, taking your 401(k) account with you to another employer).

Disclosure: The release of all information about a company that can influence a decision about investing in it.

Distribution: A payment from your retirement account — can come in installments or one lump sum.

Dollar Cost Averaging: Deducting the same amount from your paycheck each month, which means you do not have to worry as much about the fluctuating markets — you will constantly be spending the same amount each month, so that sometimes you buy high and sometimes you buy low.

Early Withdrawal Penalty: For 401(k) accounts, any money withdrawn before you reach age 59 and a half is subject to a 10 percent penalty.

Eligibility: Your ability to participate in your employer's retirement plan.

Employee Benefits Security Administration: A division of the Department of Labor that protects benefits given to employees by their employers, and helps workers understand and receive necessary information on any benefits they are eligible for through their employers.

Employee Retirement Income Security Act (ERISA): Sets minimum standards employers must follow if they offer retirement plans, health plans or pensions to their employees and former employees.

Employee Stock Ownership Plan (ESOPs): In an employee stock ownership plan, the employer gives company stock to employees. Employees do not buy or hold the stock.

Employee Stock Option Plan: The ability of an employee to purchase stock from the company he or she works for at a set price over a certain amount of time.

Equities: A security that represents ownership in a company (for example, stocks).

Excess Aggregate Contributions: Contributions made after tax, or employer matching contributions, that cause a company to fail IRS actual contribution percentage test.

Facts and Circumstances Test: A test used to determine whether you are able to make a hardship withdrawal.

Fidelity Bond: If the fiduciary or anyone else responsible for your plan steals any of the funds or does not make investments the way you asked, etc., the fiduciary bond will protect you.

Fiduciary: The person with the responsibility for making financial choices regarding your retirement account that benefit you and others in your plan rather than him or herself and your company, for example.

Fiduciary Responsibility: Anyone with a decision-making role in your 401(k) plan's investments is legally bound to make those decisions in the best interests of the plan participants (you and your coworkers), not in the best interest of the company, the plan provider, or anyone else.

Form 1099R: A form indicating the amount you received in a distribution that is filed with the IRS.

Form 5500: All qualified plans — except for SEPs and SIMPLE IRAs — must file this form yearly with the IRS.

Full Retirement Age: Full retirement age is currently 65.

Growth Stocks: Stocks that have a perceived potential for high capital appreciation, equating to higher earnings for stockholders.

Guaranteed Investment Contracts (GIC): An investment that returns a fixed rate and is held through an insurance company.

Hardship Withdrawal: An early withdrawal made from a retirement account that occurs when the account holder experiences proven financial hardship. Penalties and taxes are applied to this type of withdrawal.

Highly Compensated: An employee who owns more than 5 percent of the company they work for, or, for the previous year, earned more than $100,000 (if this is 2008; $105,000 if the year is 2009). Highly compensated employees have restrictions placed on them by the IRS as to how much they can contribute to a 401(k) plan so as to keep it fair for everyone.

Income Stocks: Low- to moderate-risk stocks, often held in stable industries such as telecommunications or utilities.

Inflation: The rise in prices of goods and services over time.

Internal Revenue Service (IRS): The arm of the U.S. Treasury that is responsible for administering retirement plan and pension rules.

Keogh Plan: Allows self-employed people to contribute to a retirement account that is defined contribution.

KSOP: A plan with 401(k) contributions and an employee stock plan.

Large-Cap Stocks: Market capitalization higher than $10 billion.

Lump Sum Distribution: Receiving one payment for all of the money in your retirement plan.

Market Capitalization: The value of a company determined by the market price of its outstanding stock and the number of stocks it has outstanding.

Matching Contribution: A contribution made by the retirement account holder's employer into the account, by and large as a percentage of what the employee contributes to his or her retirement account or a percentage of the employee's pay.

Mid-Cap Stocks: Market capitalization between $2 billion and $10 billion.

Money Market Fund: A mutual fund with holdings in short-term securities.

Monte Carlo Analysis: Repeated random sampling done through the use of computer analytics.

Multi-employer Plan: Using collective bargaining agreements, this plan is contributed to by two or more employers.

Mutual Fund: An investment that pools together money from multiple investors to be able to invest in different securities such as stocks, bonds, money market funds, and other asset classes. The fund manager invests the money in a way that ensures the fund is working to produce capital gains for those invested. A prospectus details how your mutual funds are performing. Mutual funds are especially helpful for investors putting less money into the account because it allows them to get hold of professionally managed funds without having to pay high fees or invest vast amounts of money. In a mutual fund each investor shares proportionally in the buying and selling of investments as well as the performance of each investment.

National Association of Securities Dealers Automated Quotation System (NASDAQ): The largest of the U.S. stock markets, it makes the most trades per day and has well over 3,200 companies listed on it.

New York Stock Exchange (NYSE): By dollar volume, this is considered the largest stock exchange in the world. In terms of the companies listed on this market, it falls second in the world only to NASDAQ.

Non-Highly Compensated Employee: Employees who earn less than $105,000 in 2008

Non-Qualified Plan: A retirement plan in which the premiums are not tax deductible.

Non Tax Deductible: Something that you cannot use to reduce your taxable income. (Like contributions to a Roth IRA).

Pension: A classic defined benefit plan in which the employer makes contributions to a fund and invests the money on behalf of the employee so that he or she will receive benefits from this fund in retirement. Unlike a defined contribution plan, in a defined benefit plan an employee never makes contributions to the fund.

Plan Administrator: Monitors the day-to-day activities of a 401(k) plan.

Plan Sponsor: The person who sets up a company's retirement plan and determines who may participate, what the investment options will be, and can make matching contribution payments.

Plan Year: Twelve months, calculated by calendar years, fiscal years, or another measure.

Pre-tax: Any contributions made to your retirement account that are deducted before taxes are taking from your paycheck.

Price/Book Ratio: An equation that compares a stock's market value to its book price. Calculated by dividing stock price by total assets.

Price/Earnings Ratio: Market value per share divided by earnings per share.

Profit Sharing Plan: A program through which an employer shares the company's profits with the company's employees. Normally, the amount an employee receives is based on a percentage of the profits, the employee's salary, and his or her time with the company.

Qualified Domestic Relations Order (QDRO): A court order that says you must give all or a part of your retirement account to whomever is named—husband, wife, child, etc.

Qualified Joint and Survivor Annuity (QJSA): An annuity in which, upon your death, the payments automatically rollover to your spouse, and are equal to at least 50 percent of what you were receiving.

Qualified Plan: A retirement plan that allows interest to grow tax-free or tax-deferred.

Re-characterization: Treating a contribution to an IRA plan like it was contributed to another IRA and not the one initially contributed to.

Required Minimum Distributions (RMD): The IRS requires that you begin making withdrawals from your 401(k) account when you turn 70 and a half. You must make withdrawals each year after that. The amount you must withdraw is based on your account balance and life expectancy.

Rollover: Moving investments from one retirement account to another.

Roth 401(k): A retirement savings account combining the benefits of the Roth IRA account with those of the 401(k) account.

Roth IRA: A retirement savings plan directed to high-income earners who are unable to participate in employer-sponsored retirement plans. The contributions made to the fund grow tax-free and withdrawals are tax-free as long as the account holder meets certain criteria. Contributions are not tax deductible.

Safe Harbor Rules: Allows some people or companies to be exempt from regulations.

Schedule SSA: A form filed with the federal government that deals with vesting status.

Salary Deferral: A form from your employer stating how much you elect to set aside from your pre-tax salary and put into your retirement account.

Securities: The multitude of investments offered including stocks, bonds, and mutual funds, just to name a few.

Simplified Employee Pension Plan: A retirement plan that can be established by an employer or someone who is self-employed that allows the person to make a tax deduction for all contributions to the plan.

Savings Incentive Match Plan for Employees IRA (SIMPLE IRA): A savings option for the self-employed. This type of account is normally for small businesses and it takes a percentage or set dollar amount from the employee's paycheck as contributions.

Small-Cap Stocks: Market capitalization between $300 million and $2 billion.

Stock Bonus Plan: DC plan with matching contributions made through company stock.

Summary Plan Description: A document detailing a retirement plan, including who is able to participate in the plan.

Target Benefit Plan: Similar to a defined benefit plan, but the benefits cannot be guaranteed because they are based on the performance of the funds investments.

Tax Deductible: Something that can reduce your taxable income.

Top Heavy Plan: A retirement plan that benefits highly-compensated employees or owners of the company.

Traditional IRA: A retirement account in which contributions can be either tax deductible or non-tax deductible. Any interest in the account grows tax-deferred and withdrawals are taxable, unless the withdrawal comes from the non-tax deductible portion of the account.

Trustee: A bank or investment company with fiduciary responsibility who acts in the stead of your employer to upkeep and monitor your 401(k) account.

Vesting: A time period after which the employee receives the rights to employer contributions to his or her 401(k) plan.

Vesting Schedule: The time frame in which an employee becomes fully vested in the employer contributions offered by his or her retirement plan.

Index